CORRUPTION
OFFICER

CORRUPTION OFFICER

From Jail Guard to Perpetrator
Inside Rikers Island

GARY L. HEYWARD

ATRIA PAPERBACK

NEW YORK   LONDON   TORONTO   SYDNEY   NEW DELHI

ATRIA PAPERBACK

A Division of Simon & Schuster, Inc.
1230 Avenue of the Americas
New York, NY 10020

First Atria Paperback edition March 2015

ATRIA PAPERBACK and colophon are trademarks of Simon & Schuster, Inc.

For information about special discounts for bulk purchases, please contact Simon &
Schuster Special Sales at 1-866-506-1949 or business@simonandschuster.com.

The Simon & Schuster Speakers Bureau can bring authors to your live event. For more
information or to book an event, contact the Simon & Schuster Speakers Bureau at
1-866-248-3049 or visit our website at www.simonspeakers.com.

Interior design by Paul Dippolito

Manufactured in the United States of America

10   9   8   7   6   5   4   3   2

Library of Congress Cataloging-in-Publication Data
    Heyward, Gary L.
        Corruption officer : from jail guard to perpetrator inside Rikers Island /
    Gary L. Heyward.
            pages cm
        Summary: "In this shocking memoir from a former corrections officer,
    Gary Heyward shares an eye-opening, gritty, and devastating account of his
    descent into criminal life, smuggling contraband inside the infamous
    Rikers Island jails"—Provided by publisher.
        1. Smugglers—New York (State)—New York—Biography. 2. Criminals—
    New York (State)—New York—Biography. 3. Correctional personnel—
    New York (State)—New York—Biography. 4. Rikers Island (N.Y.) I. Title.
        HJ6647.H49A3 2015
        365'.64092—dc23
        [B]
                                            2014041036
ISBN 978-1-4767-9432-7
ISBN 978-1-4767-9433-4 (ebook)

DEDICATION AND ACKNOWLEDGMENTS

First and foremost I would like to thank God; without Him nothing is possible.

I would like to dedicate this book to my family:

To my loving wife, Tondalaya Heyward, who believed in me when I was at the lowest point in my life and for putting up with me, because I know that I am "no walk in the park." Love you always.

To my mother, Christine Heyward, my rock, thank you for always being there for me no matter what. I apologize for putting you through all this; you and I both know that you raised me to know better.

To my son, Gary Jr., and my daughter, Porsha, I hope that you can take the things that I have done—good and bad—and learn what to do and what not to do. I love you both dearly.

To my sister, Joyce aka Big Bunny! Thanks for always understanding my points of view but not being afraid to let me know when I am wrong.

To Johnny Mann Sr., aka Uncle Robert, thanks for everything—for your motivational talks, for always supporting me in everything that I did, and especially for loaning me your suit, tie, and shoes to go on job interviews. Things like that are priceless.

To my nephews, Alex and Dawud, I am proud of both of you. Keep following your dreams and being the true Heywards that you are; don't let nobody tell you anything different.

DEDICATION AND ACKNOWLEDGMENTS

To my brother, Terrance, and two sisters, Na-Na and Mo-Mo, and to all of my family in the South. I love you all.

To the "Good Money Brothers!" Fredrick Edwards, aka Black Fred, Carl Joseph Sr., Rapper Cashflow (Carl Joseph Jr), and Joe Hunter—they don't make them like you guys no more! Thanks for the love and support for my grind to get this book done!

To my longtime best friend, Anthony Johnson, thanks for being there for me from day one. Never had an argument or disagreement in over forty years of friendship.

I would like to thank:

Atria Books and my editor, Todd Hunter, for guiding me, listening to my voice, not taking me out of my book, being supportive of my views, and most of all, being patient with me.

Sister Souljah for everything she's done to get me here.

To my neighborhood (Polo Grounds projects), thank you for looking out for me. When I was on parole and had to be in the house by 9:00 p.m., everyone knew it, so at 8:30 p.m. I would get all kinds of warnings from my friends. No matter where I would be, they would tap their watches at this time, indicating to me that it was time for me to get my butt upstairs! To me, that's love.

And to my coworkers and anyone else I did not mention—thanks for the love and support!

AUTHOR'S NOTE

Everything that I've written inside this book is true and recounted to the best of my ability.

The events that occur in *Corruption Officer* happened over a period of my life while I was employed as a corrections officer at Rikers Island. I wrote this book while serving time as a convicted felon for smuggling drugs and other contraband inside the jails.

At its core, this book serves to enlighten others about what can happen to you if you break the law and get caught. Having been convicted, I know that my story can be used to help other officers who are now corrupt or considering doing something illegal. I know no one is actively reaching out to corrections officers about what happens when you get caught for corruption. I'm aware of the arrogance of many within the Corrections Department who think they will not get caught for corruption or that they are above the law. But let my story show that there are consequences for corruption. I know. I've now lived on both sides of the law. Jail is a bad, bad place.

Some of the names inside the book have been changed. It is not my intent to put an officer's business in the streets, nor is it to blatantly bad-mouth the Corrections Department.

Ultimately, *Corruption Officer* is a symbol of my second chance. When I was convicted, I never thought I would be in this place, an author at a major publishing house, telling my story for all to read. This is my opportunity to help others and to right my wrongs. This is my blessing.

CORRUPTION OFFICER

CHAPTER 1

THE G-SPOT

"HEAD CRACK!" the houseman yelled.

"Alright, nobody move!" he said, as he went around the table to collect the money from the bettors.

The game was C-low and at this time my man Fungler was at the top of his game again. It's a Friday night, payday, and I have every dime in the bank (the bank is the guy who takes the money for bets) on Fungler. I gave him that name because that's what he yells every time he shoots the dice. I'm his hype, motivating him when he shoots and antagonizing the other bettors around the table to bet against him. Whenever he'd win we both made money. Lately Fungler was on a roll.

Fungler and I would be on our bullshit as usual. When Fungler would get the dice he'd shuffle them, then shake them in his hand. I'd be beside him screaming, "Thrilla in the manila dilla!" He'd shake his head indicating "no." Then I'd scream, "Feva in the Funkhouse!" He'd shake his head again indicating "no." Then I'd scream, "Rumble in the Jungle." Then Fungler would say, "Rumble in the jungle without the fungle kungle," while simultaneously releasing the dice and watching them register. Every time we did this routine, we'd hear the houseman yell, "HEAD CRACK!"

People who had bet against him would put their heads down or have the shit-face (upset facial expressions). Then a cheerleader from the side would yell, "Double or nothing, I bet he can't do it again!" A cheerleader is a person on the sidelines with no money, talking shit about somebody else's money! Fungler gets the dice, but before we go into our routine, in walks Chuck.

Chuck's money is long. He has a lot of it. Every time Chuck comes in, muthafuckas who are scared, and have the bank with a lot of money in it, normally pass it to the next bettor. They don't want to take a chance of losing it all in one shot. Everybody knows Chuck will stop up your bank—putting a large amount of money down on a bet equal to or more than what you have.

Everybody knows the routine, but not Fungler. Fungler's eyes lit up. He hollered at Chuck, "Get down, nigga. I know you ain't come here to sightsee!" Fungler looked at me with a shit-eatin' grin like, "I got this nigga!" I looked at him like, "Muthafucka, just pass the bank!" Then somebody on the side said, "Look at this STD (scared-to-death) ass nigga!" and everybody laughed.

Yes, scared ass nigga, a person who tries to gamble with the big dawgs but really has a low-paying security job, and has no business being at the gambling spot in Harlem, or anywhere else for that matter, 'cause he knows that he is living PTP (paycheck to paycheck). If he loses his money this payday Friday night, he will be like Sidney Poitier in *A Raisin in the Sun* when Willie runs off with all that money.

"Willie, don't do it, Willie, not with that money, Willie!"

Yes, scared nigga. That would be me! Gary, Gee, Big Hey. It all depends on who is calling me. My momma calls me "Boy" or "Nutmo," aka scared nigga!

So Chuck dropped his stack. And Fungler started talking shit, saying, "After this roll all you working niggas are going to be sick!

You're gonna throw up on your way to the ATM! I love taking a nine-to-five nigga's money, but taking a hustler's money is like winning ten thousand dollars on one of those scratch tickets. What is that?" Fungler asked the crowd.

"FREE MONEY!" everybody replied.

Everybody except me. I was busy trying to get this nigga's attention to pass that muthafuckin' bank! Fungler continued to shake the dice, ridiculing Chuck.

"Taking a hustler's money is like going to Rent-A-Center, getting a whole bunch of shit delivered to your apartment, then moving to Brooklyn!"

Again, everybody laughed, except me. I was still in scared nigga mode!

"Getting his money is like going up in a bitch raw dog and not worrying about kids 'cause she got her tubes tied!" Fungler continued, and said, "What's that?"

"FREE MONEY!!" They all laughed.

I'm over here figuratively sharting on myself, like when you think you have to fart but mistakenly shit on yourself instead. Chuck screamed out, "Nigga, would you stop walking the cat walk and just roll the muthafuckin' dice!" Fungler shook them, then looked at me. Man, listen, the look I gave him was not a confident one. I did not even play with this nigga.

"Fungle in the rumble jungle kungle without the ungle dungle sungle?" I screamed out. *Whatever the fuck that meant.*

Fungler threw the dice. It seemed like it took an eternity as they flew past my face. At that moment all I could think about was my kids asking me for Michael Jordan sneakers, my past-due rent. Mom Dukes ain't taking no shorts on rent. If I lose, how am I going to get to work next week? Willie, don't do it!

The dice hit the wall and registered one-one-six! Fungler screamed, "HEAD CRACK!" I momentarily blacked out, then came back screaming, "NIIII-ZZIIIII-GAA!" After the house collected the money, totaling about sixty-six hundred dollars, I went over to Fungler and copped out, saying, "Yo, man, I gotta go." So Fungler passed the bank. We split the dough. I tore the door off its hinges getting the fuck out of there.

CHAPTER 2

STEP UP MY GAME

I called my man C to come pick me up.

"Hennimus Dogumus?" he says on the other end of the phone.

That's our Greek name for Hennessy.

"Yeaaah, maan!" I say.

And automatically he says, "Oh, my God, this nigga must have cracked them niggas at the g-spot." Well, I could not take the credit for Fungler's work, so I was honest and told him.

"Hell yeah, nigga, you know how I do!" I said.

You see, C was my right-hand man and he always warned me about me having the shakes—an addictive gambling problem. He was there when I won and there when I lost.

"I'll be there in fifteen minutes," he said.

While I was waiting, I saw a friend of mine named Fredis. He ran the g-spot and knew me since I was a youngster. He came over to me and playfully said, "Let me hold something before the hoes get you!" I knew he was joking 'cause he was another get-money Harlem cat whose pockets stayed fat. Me, I wasn't a Harlem cat. I was just, ah . . . um, a person that lived in Harlem. I jokingly told him that he was too late because this money was already spent last week. He gave me dap, and while I was waiting for C we reminisced on when

I first came to the gambling spot. Back then, I rarely had money. I used to just come to watch all the hustlers, scammers, and real Harlem thugs gamble. It would be a smoke-filled room with weed and anything else you wanted to smoke. Everybody had an MO or a hustle. There you had credit card scammers, pickpockets, and real live pimps with perms, rollers in their hair, and all. I would just sit there and listen to the tales of who's making the most money and who fell off. I got to know a lot of people and they became my illegitimate family. I learned and I witnessed everything. Females would come in there looking good, all dressed up, and dudes would try to holla, but these chicks were about their business. They were professional boosters. I mean from hair spray to expensive mink coats, you could get it at the g-spot.

I remember one time I was hanging out there and Fredis asked me to go with him to one of his other spots—a crack house. I was about fifteen years old, and Fredis always looked out for me. So I went with him there to drop off some stuff. We arrive and all I see is about five or six guys, some sitting, some standing—all getting blowjobs. I was like, "Oh, shit!" I was shocked. I was still a virgin. Fredis saw the look on my face and without me knowing pushed me out into the middle of the room. I tried to play it off like, "Nah, I'm cool," but they wouldn't let me walk. So this chick, who was not a bad-looking crackhead, proceeded to give me a blowjob. Little did anybody know, it was my first one. Some dudes would be traumatized that an older woman touched them, but in my hood I'd hear young dudes saying stuff like, "Yo, Miss Peterson sucked your dick, too?" They'd laugh, give each other dap, and say, "I'm going back tomorrow, and she'll make sandwiches."

Back in those days, 1986, '87, crack hit the streets hard. Whew! I remember Fredis and a bunch of other guys in the neighborhood had all the fine chicks in the projects. They would not give a young brother, like myself, any play, knowing that my only source of income was a summer youth job. What happened to that program?

I would try to impress the fly girls though. I remember taking a kitchen knife with me to the armory on 139th Street to get my paycheck and then risking my neck to go to a Jew-man's store that sold the latest sneakers for cheap. The knife was for the people waiting outside the store to rob you. But when crack hit, it was like freaknik up in those burnt-out buildings. Every time one of those fly chicks slipped and got strung out, news traveled like a police blotter.

EXTRA! EXTRA! LISA FROM BUILDING 1 WITH THE FAT ASS THAT USED TO DATE CARLOS IS OPEN!

With five dollars and a dream all a young dude's fantasies would come true.

When C pulls up, we bounce to the liquor store not far from where we are. We got some Hennimus and park in the "office"—this is where we go to have real talk, the corner of 155th Street and Eighth Avenue, in front of the supermarket. C was a state corrections officer and he was always telling me that I had to step up my job game. I was working as a security guard, one step up from a summer youth job. Security work was year-round, though. I told him that I had taken several city and state job tests and was still looking. I'd been looking ever since I came home from the marines as a Gulf War veteran. Yeah, I know what you're thinking . . . a Gulf War veteran and you're only a security guard.

CHAPTER 3

THE LETTER

C dropped me off at my building. We had agreed to meet up later to hit a club. I ran into Junebug, a local crackhead, on my way into my building. Junebug would fix anything for you—a TV, a typewriter, a radio, anything. He asked if I wanted to buy some batteries. He assured me that he had had them for a year and that they were still good because he kept wrapping them with aluminum foil and putting them in a refrigerator. I wondered, *Nigga, you live in the streets. Where's the fridge?* I bought them from him anyway, mainly because officially he was my cousin from my mother's side of the family. I already had my own batteries wrapped in aluminum foil in my fridge, which had lasted me three years. Not many people in the neighborhood knew Junebug was my cousin. Sometimes it's embarrassing to have a family member strung out on crack, but then in my neighborhood who didn't have a family member who was a part of this epidemic? My brother died from the drug while I was in the military. So, after I copped the batteries with the lifetime warranty, I proceeded to get on the only elevator out of six that was still working.

As I stepped in I saw the pool of piss on the floor. The gremlins, aka kids or grown-ups who piss in the elevator and spit on the buttons so you could not press your floor, were hard at work. I often wondered why the military was wasting time trying to find Saddam Hussein when they should be trying to catch these muthafuckas. Well, anyway, I got Junebug to press the button for my floor, the elevator door closed, and it started up. Then it jumped, stopped, then started up again, going at a snail's pace. All I could do was curse and think again about what C had told me about stepping up my job game. I knew I had to because my situation right now was crazy. I had a bullshit security job that wasn't paying much. I was married to my childhood sweetheart, who lived on the same floor as I did with my two kids around the corner. She lived with her moms and I lived with mine. I wanted a better job so I could get us an apartment and so we could act as a family. Although she and I had our differences while I was in the military, we were still willing to try.

We had a son and a daughter and I desperately needed to do something, because I grew up around here all my life. Times were changing fast. It used to be that there was a level of respect because all the muthafuckas doing the robbing and killing were the same individuals that your moms used to babysit. So it was a weird sense of comfort that you knew that your momma might get robbed but they weren't going to kill her. Nowadays these young kids don't care. Yo momma, my momma, it don't matter. Anybody can get got. The projects are something else and I knew I had to get out.

As the elevator got to my floor, before I got out, I let out a real stinky fart, a little present for the next person who's going to walk into the elevator—you know, to go along with the spit and the piss. Shit, fuck dat! Them niggas do it to me. As I was walking to my door I checked the walls for the latest news of what's going on in the projects. It's always in the form of graffiti. They always had some shit like, "If you wantcha dick sucked, go see Tasha or Monique in apartment such and such." I hope I never see my daughter's name up on that wall. If I do, somebody gots to die. So, after scraping the bottom of my feet on the hallway floor, my best attempt to get the piss off the bottom of my shoes, I entered my mother's apartment. Yes, I was living with Mom Dukes at the age of twenty-nine. Man, I wanted to get out. I was trying.

As per usual, I put down my things and proceed to look in the pots to see what she cooked.

"Boy, go and wash your hands," she yells from the back of the apartment.

I know not to stop at a fast-food joint, 'cause my momma cooks. If I slipped up and brought home some sautéed cat soufflé from the local Chinese joint, I would definitely get the beat-down like Willie.

"Don't do it, Willie. Don't do it!" Just a little thing we used to say.

"You got some mail," she said.

I went over to the table to see which bill collector was requesting my attention, and that's when shit started to change. I got a letter from Corrections stating that I was to start at the Academy on July 10. That was 1997. After I read the letter, I was hyped. Things were finally changing for the better.

My situation now: I had about three thousand dollars in my pocket. I only had three hundred dollars and change from my paycheck before the g-spot. Now I had ten times that amount. That's the way it was at the g-spot, you could either be a thousandaire or you could end up hanging yourself in a matter of fifteen minutes. So here I was with my three stacks and the batteries I copped from Junebug. I'd already wrapped them and put them in the freezer behind the smoked neckbones.

So I ran to my momma and sat on her lap—all 260 pounds of me. She screamed, "Boy, if you don't get off of me!" All I could do was show her the letter from the Department of Corrections, and when she read it she jumped up, screaming out loud, "You did it!" I mean me and my momma hugged and danced around the living room. We did the robot, the snake, the Patty Duke, and then she went and did the Watusi (she lost me there). Then she came back with the roach stomper. We both did this very well because we had a lot of practice.

After we danced I went to take a shower to go hang out with C. After I got out I went to my closet, which consisted of my brother's military uniforms (he was a marine, God bless him) and a whole bunch of other stuff that wasn't mine. There was only a small space for my clothes. You know at twenty-nine you ain't supposed to be staying at your mom's. You're supposed to be there just long enough to get on your feet and then get your own place. Well, my small space had all my outfits for partying. I had a Chinese mock neck and a pair of those slacks with the checkered design, the ice-cubed slacks. Seriously, I had thirty different shirts and one pair of black pants. When I went out I would switch my shirts up and wear the same black pants. In the dark, who's going to notice? So I grabbed the one and only Versace shirt, which took me three paychecks to purchase, but I got it. Yeah, nigga what? My Versace shirt and my never-let-me-down black pants.

I was getting dressed, thinking about my new job as a corrections officer. I looked in the mirror and at this time my mother came to the door of the bathroom and we started discussing what this meant. My mother broke it down to me that Corrections was a good job and there were so many things that I could accomplish with it. I could find an apartment and really give my marriage a try. And though my wife and I hadn't really been together in a while and the feelings weren't there anymore, the idea sounded nice. My mother went on to say that the benefits were good for my kids, Gary Junior and Porsha. They could grow up in a better environment once I saved up to get a house. She went on to say how she was proud that I stayed out of trouble, went into the marines, served in the Gulf War, and now landed this job. She hugged me and I saw her eyes swell up in tears because she just wanted the best for me and to see me do good. Ain't nothing like Mom Dukes.

If you are reading this book and right now you and your moms is beefing . . . make up with her, because you only get one. (Message.)

After I got dressed I called C and told him I'd meet him downstairs. I had yet to tell him about my made-man status. Yes, made man. In the ghetto everybody knows that if you land a city or state job you hold on to that job, you do your twenty years and retire young, depending on your age when you start. The made status goes as follows: 1) consistent money, never worrying when or where your next check is coming from; 2) consistent coochie, the chicks that would not give the "one step up from a summer job" brother a look, are now constantly dropping the draws because of BEN-O-FITS; and 3) the perks, everybody in the hood will now know that nigga got a gun and a muthafucking badge. Traffic stops—whip out the badge—BAM. Bouncer at the club—stop—BAM! Subway and bus—BAM! Chicks putting up a coochie stop sign—BAM! BAM! HA HA! I felt like Master P in the projects because the badge sometimes had NO LIMITS.

I met C downstairs and we went back to the liquor store, you know, to preflight before we got to the club. It was after twelve when we arrived, so the store was closing and the Indian dude would not let me in.

If I had my badge, BAM! He'd let me in.

C and I went to the Chinese restaurant/number-hole spot or place where people play illegal numbers, the ghetto OTB, and I don't mean Old Tenement Building. It was a place where you could get liquor after-hours. What? Don't act like there are no bootleggers in your hood. After I got the McFinister aka Hennessy we jetted to the club. On the way there I told C about me becoming a CO and he was like, "Ooooh shit! These chicks better lock their coochies up!"

"Ya know that's right. Do they still make chastity belts?" I asked.

"Yeah. Now they are more up to date. They have combination locks on them," he said.

We both laughed. As C and I drove to the club I thought to myself that this job wasn't about chicks or perks, it was about survival. It was about me doing whatever I had to do to take care of my family.

CHAPTER 4

THE ACADEMY

"Eighteen hundred dollars! Eighteen hundred dollars! Boy, I know you're out of your mind! Coming here asking me for that kind of money! You might as well walk back out that door and, here, take my garbage out while you at it!"

I needed the money to buy uniforms for the Academy. I knew it was a long shot coming here to my uncle Robert's house asking for his help. I mean, this was my uncle Robert, the closest thing to a father figure I had. I am not saying that I did not know my real father, it's just that my uncle was always there for my family, ever since I was little. He did whatever he could for my moms and us and she'd do the same for him.

Uncle Robert was my last resort. I had already exhausted all my other options.

Everything else I'd needed to do to get into the Academy had been smooth sailing. Well, almost everything. I'd just finished filling out all my background investigation paperwork for the second time. The Application Unit called me a day before I was supposed to report for duty informing me that the investigator assigned to me hadn't done the investigation. They said that if I wanted the job I had to come down there and fill out all the paperwork all over again. A day before I was supposed to report. Some investigation.

I reported for my first two days at the Academy in proper business attire for orientation. Now I'm back standing here in front of Uncle Robert in his blazer, his white shirt, his tie (I had my own black slacks that I used for clubbing—ya know, the old reliable), and his shoes, asking for his help once again for uniform money. I had already spent my check at the gambling spot, hoping I could pull another miracle and come up with the money on my own like I did the other night. Unfortunately, the gambling gods were not with me. I lost almost all my money, except for train fare to get me back and forth to the Academy. I didn't even have lunch money, which is why I was at my uncle Robert's house.

My uncle was standing there looking like himself with his sweat pants, no socks, no shirt, and his penny loafers. He always told me that his loafers, nobody else's, only his, were official because they had real pennies in them. So I really needed Uncle Robert to look out for me.

Standing there I'm thinking to myself, *With this job I can finally get my grown man on again.*

"Boy, let me tell you . . ." my uncle began.

I knew the speech was coming. I had only heard it a million times and here comes a million and one.

"You need to get your shit together," he said. "I know you've been trying to get a better job since you got out of the military, so if you land this you'd better make the best of it."

Then he said, like a father would say to his son, "When do you need it by?"

"Yesterday," I said.

After my uncle and I made arrangements on how I was going to pay him back he said for me to make sure I paid him on time, because if I didn't somebody was going to come up missing.

Then, just before I left him, he said, "Put my clothes in the cleaner's before you return them and, boy, take this garbage out."

The next day my uncle and I went to get my uniforms. Yes, he came with me. He wasn't going to spend all that money if he did not have to. We bought only what I needed to start the Academy and that's all.

CHAPTER 5

FIRST DAY AT THE ACADEMY

At 5:00 a.m. I was on the M train taking it to the last stop, Metropolitan Avenue. That's where the Academy was located. It was a ninety-degree day in July. I was sweating because I was in full uniform with a jacket on for cover. It was an Academy rule that corrections recruits are not supposed to wear their uniforms in the streets without covering them up. Why? Because yo fool ass is not a cop. If you are seen and somebody asks you for help, what are you going to do then, mister corrections officer? Nothing. Because ya ass is just a recruit!

The train was funky because a bum was on it straight stinking it up. I covered my nose and sat there thinking of all the trains that I had to take to get to the Academy. The D to the J to the M. Shiiiiit! I gots to get me a ride, because a nigga ain't going to be getting up crazy early to take fifty trains from Harlem just to get here on time. Negro ain't been on the job a hot week and already complaining about what he ain't going to do.

As I sat there a fat woman was sitting across from the bum eating a bagel. The bum stared at her as she took her time eating and licking her fingers. She looked at him, rolled her eyes, and continued to eat. Then out of nowhere the bum jumped up and grabbed what was left of the fat chick's bagel right out of her hand. She leaned back away from him in shock. He leaned forward close to her face and proceeded to stuff the food in his mouth, cream cheese and all. The train came to a stop, the doors opened, and he strolled out looking at her with a smile of satisfaction. She then looked around, eyes wide in search for somebody, anybody that could possibly help her. Her eyes locked on me. I gave her a look like, "What do you want me to do?"

"Ain't you going to the Academy?" she asked me.

I guess she saw the dark blue uniform pants and my uncle's patent-leather shoes that I shined up with Vaseline.

"Nope, I'm a security guard," I said.

Academy rule number one, no police contact of any kind while you are on probation. *Humph. Just my luck I play superhero and jam myself right out of a job. No, sir, not me, not I, said the cat. Fuck outta here. Besides, bums gotta eat, too.*

When I arrived at the Academy, I was placed in an area somewhat like a gymnasium. All kinds of equipment were lined up on the side, helmets, stab-proof vests, and floor mats. We were broken up into groups called squads. As I stood there among the other recruits, I noticed that we all had the same look on our faces. *I need this job, man!* The first day there we were put in classrooms and briefed on rules and regulations. They told us stuff like when we graduated and went to work in the jails we would be put on a schedule called "the wheel." This meant that our work hours would rotate from week to week. "The end of the world as you know it," they'd tell us. You're not going to know whether you're coming or going, and your sleeping patterns are going to be all fucked up, 7:00 a.m. to 3:00 p.m., 3:00 p.m. to 11:00 p.m., 11:00 p.m. to 7:00 a.m., then flip mode, 11:00 in the morning until 7:00 p.m. and shit. All sorts of fucked-up hours. I don't even want to begin with the four o' clock in the morning tours. You can forget partying every weekend. Little did I know at the time, but COs party Monday to Monday. Female recruits were warned to get a backup babysitter for the backup babysitter. Lack of a babysitter is no reason to miss work. In my CO career, there were several female officers reprimanded by Child Welfare for leaving under-aged children at home alone. Some female recruits frowned with attitudes, and the instructor kindly gave them the look like, "Do you want this job? You can always go back to the supermarket."

We were also warned not to fraternize with our coworkers. Tah! The instructor might as well have been Charlie Brown's teacher, "Wa-womp wa-womp womp wooommp," because muthafuckas exchanged numbers with those chicks faster than you can say "Booty!" Then the instructor ended the day's lessons by announcing that tomorrow we were going to Rikers Island! That's when everybody got quiet and deep in thought.

The looks on some recruits' faces told it all:

Do I really want to do this shit?

I am a female.

Are they really going to put me in there with Big Luke and Murder and them?

Dang, this is our first week. Are they going to really throw us to the wolves like that?

One female recruit was staring into space chewing her gum and licking her lips. Then she stuck her tongue out and touched the bottom of her chin. I knew then that she was going to be alright in a jail full of men, or a jail full of women for that matter.

After the announcement all the horror stories started to circulate, like the one about the female officer who fell asleep on post in a dorm area and the inmates took turns jerking off and nutting on her face. She woke up and all her acne was gone. Or the inmate who filled up a tube of toothpaste with his own shit and squirted it into an officer's face. That one shook the shit out of me. I thought to myself, *Yeah, I would definitely lose my job.* Damn the getting out of the projects and the better life for my kids. If a nigga splash, squirt, shoot anything in my muthafuckin' face . . . I don't even want to talk about it. Then we heard the story of these famous Chinese brothers that kicked everybody's ass, including the warden's. I thought about how many people I was going to see over there from the streets. I just hoped that I didn't see Junebug, because I threw away the batteries that I bought from him and I knew that he would ask me how they were working.

CHAPTER 6

RIKERS

The next day I arrived at Rikers Island for the very first time in my life. I always heard about it but never visited. It was just that, too, an island, right next to LaGuardia Airport. There's only one way on and one way off. There's a long bridge leading to the island that connects to a large officers' parking lot. An officer has to park his vehicle, then take what they call a route bus to his assigned jail. Visitors have to take a public bus over to the island, then go to the main visitors' building. Then they take the various route buses to the jail they're visiting. The first jail I went to was called HDM.

HDM or House of Detention for Men was the first jail ever to be built on Rikers Island. This is back when the commissary was called the trade post. It had the Alcatraz look, the old worn-out metal, the rusty bars, and then there was the smell. Guuaad damn! It's a combination of funky sweat, funky asses, and three-day-old cabbage that's been sitting out.

I reported for roll call, where a supervisor ran off officers' names, checked attendance, and made announcements. You could tell who the new officers were because we were standing at the end of the line with our Academy uniforms and black patent-leather wedding cake shoes. We were standing there, eyes bright, hearts pumping with anticipation of what was in store for us that day. Senior officers who had been on the job a while looked and chuckled at us. Some just leaned against the wall half-ass listening to what was being said with a look of *Hurry the fuck up with this bullshit*. The new officers were assigned to certain posts for training. We walked through long corridors looking stupid, searching for signs and certain numbers that might tell us where the fuck we were supposed to be going. As we walked by, officers looked at us like we were lambs going to the slaughter. Others took the time out to help us with directions, or so we thought.

"You got to go down this hall to cell block 37. Then make a right until you come to a door. Knock on the door three times and ask for Officer Cocks. He'll show you where to go." Yeah, they had their fun with us.

I got to the gate where I was supposed to work and a female officer let me in the first gate, then gestured for me to enter another gate. Then, boom! The gate slammed behind me and I shitted on myself. *Great, now I have to walk around here all day with soiled underwear, squishing with every step I take. Damn!* When I went inside, there was a long galleyway that seemed to go on forever. There were inmates on the second and third tier looking down on me, laughing at my shoes.

This is about the time that reality sets in. All the stories you've heard about jail, all the fear of getting punched in your face or worse, seem all too real. It's like some people's first day of high school. That level of anxiety comes right back in a moment. And I ask myself, "Do I really want this job?" Since I was six-foot-two and 260 pounds of Hennessy and oxtails, I tried to swell my chest out to impress them. The inmates were not impressed. One inmate said, "Look at this doofy muthafucka!" They laughed. Then another inmate said, "Ain't you glad you don't have to flip burgers no more?" I just continued to walk down the galley looking for the officer that I was assigned to work with. Inmates were everywhere doing push-ups, hanging on the bars doing pull-ups, each either laughing at me or ice grilling me. Either way, I was starting to get the feeling that all I wanted to do was get the fuck out of there.

Inmates were all around me as I continued to walk. A huge inmate about six-four, maybe four hundred pounds, approached me and gave me a folded piece of paper. He stated that I would need these because I did not have any. Confused, I opened the paper and it was a drawing of a man's balls. Again they laughed. That was it. I had had enough. *Fuck this job!* With my heart pumping, sweat and Jheri curl juice dripping down my forehead, I was about to make a beeline toward the gate to get the fuck out of there! Then my conscience came into play: *Negro, you need this job. Man up! What about your family, your kids?* As I held that note in my hand looking up at this towering inmate, I thought, *Fuck the kids! I am out.* Then I thought, *You're going to let this big nigga stop you from getting all that pussy this job has to offer? Oh, hell no!*

With my priorities in the right place, I mustered up some testicles and was about to handle this big nigga—yeah, right—when all my tormentors yelled out simultaneously, "Ohh, shit! Here comes the CO!" *What the fuck was I, then?* Then they parted like the Red Sea. I looked ahead, expecting some seven-foot-ten-inch corrections officer, when out of the crowd walked this 105-pound, four-foot-something female. She had salt-and-pepper hair and a pair of glasses that she wore on her nose.

"Back the fuck up!" she yelled.

They did. She then grabbed me by my arm and led me away from the crowd. I looked like a kid that got his ass beat, whose momma had to take him away from all the other kids at the playground. She then yelled at the other female officer who had let me in.

"Ooooh, girl, they sent me a big one this time. That's fabulous," she said.

An inmate yelled out from the upper tier, "Look at that nigga's gut. You mean more like Flabulous!" The inmates laughed loud and hard.

The rest of the day went pretty much like that, and when it was over, I tore the gate off its hinges getting the fuck out of there.

CHAPTER 7

UNDUE FAMILIARITY

For the next couple of days we went back to the Academy, and classes went on, with boring instructors telling us the dos and don'ts of being a corrections officer Academy-style. They told us not to mess around with the inmates, emphasizing that we would jeopardize our jobs by bringing things to inmates or fraternizing with them in any way. The instructors told us point-blank that these individuals (the inmates) don't care about you or your family. They don't have anything to do all day but scheme on you. They focus on what they can get from you or what they can get you to do for them. Then the instructors gave us all kinds of examples of how we could get into trouble, like undue familiarity. Let me explain. You're now a corrections officer. You now have peace officer status. Whoooo! You now have just a teensy bit more police power than the average Joe. As an almighty corrections officer you're going to be held in high regard and expected to uphold the law, mainly in the jails but also to some extent on the streets as well. This means that your life, as you know it, is over. Juju and Toejoe, your best friends since grade school, can no longer be a part of your life if they have felonies. You're not to associate with any known felon. That means if your grandmoms was a gangster in her heyday and accumulated some felonies, by Cor-

27

rections guideline's you can no longer go visit her in the projects for Christmas. If your neighborhood is anything like mine, that would be anybody in a fifty-mile radius. That means if you are seen hanging out with people that have felonies or you're seen in pictures with said individuals, you can be brought up on charges and could possibly lose your job.

This is what didn't really make sense: How did they really expect us to turn off our feelings and emotions toward people who had been a part of our lives before we obtained this job? I knew right away that this was going to be a problem for me. I was told that officers, such as myself, who were born and raised in neighborhoods where there was a large contingent of individuals with criminal backgrounds would see at least five to ten people they knew within the first week of working in the jails. If you encounter someone that you know, you'd better see them before they see you because they will shout you out. I was told that the professional way to deal with this is to write a report to administration requesting that the inmate be moved to another facility. Again, like I said, if your neighborhood was like mine, you were going to see a lot of inmates that you knew. That's a lot of report writing, and to some officers it sort of raised a red flag as to what kind of person you were if you knew a lot of these kinds of people.

The other conventional way of handling the situation goes as follows: If you see an inmate that you know and you know that this particular individual not only knows you but knows all your dirty little secrets, you must approach this inmate and let him know that you're an officer now and that he can't expect any special treatment. If he gets loud and disrespectful then you take matters to the next level. You smack him, spray his face with mace, and yell, "Man, I told you about coming in and out of this place! Now respect my job!"

Slight exaggeration, but close to the truth. Corrections wants you to treat inmates like inmates no matter who they are. As a corrections officer you'd better learn how to balance personal life with job life or you're going to be in a world of trouble. It's simple. You got this job with the purpose of getting ahead in life and bettering your situation. People sell their souls for opportunities such as these. You have lived in the projects all your life, kept your nose clean so that when jobs like these became available, you qualified. You're in now and you're not going to blow it. Yeah, baby, just cruise the next twenty years and you're in the clear. Hello, pension!

CHAPTER 8

USE OF FORCE

The next rule that instructors gave us that I found confusing was "Use of force." This is the right-to-kick-ass rule.

They gave us different scenarios of when to use force and how much. Many of the Caucasian recruits paid close attention to this lesson, foaming at the mouth and shit.

It made sense to me that if you're working in a jail—excluding inmate employees—a hostile environment, that you should be able to defend yourself. The first thing that was said was that you should always try to defuse a hostile situation. We were to utilize our IPC (interpersonal communication) skills. Talk your way out of either giving an ass-whipping or receiving one. Either way, they wanted us to talk first. I thought to myself, *So let me get this straight, if I am working in a housing area and Jerome Thomas, aka Killa J from the group home, is standing in front of me with several bodies laid out in front of him and blood dripping from his mouth because he bit off someone's ear, I am supposed to utilize my IPC skills and say, "So, who do you think the Knicks are going to get in the trade this year?"* After all the horror stories I'd heard and after my first visit to the jail, I just couldn't grasp that they would have me talk to the inmate instead of handcuffing him to a pole and beating the spit out of him. Just kidding.

On a serious note, I did learn that you just can't go around the jail beating up on inmates for no reason, because if your Is are not dotted and your Ts are not crossed you can get in a lot of trouble. You are to use force as a last resort if everything else has failed. And by all means try to avoid a physical altercation with an inmate. *In jail? Yeah, right.*

In the following weeks we were given lessons in hand-to-hand combat. The movements were called "kodagash" and "comealong." It was bullshit training that I knew half these petite women, and men, for that matter, would never be able to use if the shit really hit the fan. Muthafuckas were fat and out of shape and using muscles that had lain dormant for years. It was kind of comical seeing them try, though, because you knew that three months of training was not going to help. Then there were the practices using fighting movements with riot gear on. This shit was bulky and awkward and it really took some getting used to before a person could maneuver in it effectively. Some of us know-it-alls felt that the gear would more likely hinder us than help us. Chicks were upset because no matter what, they had to put that helmet on. One chick had her hair up in a bouffant like Marge Simpson and she had to put the helmet on. Adding insult to injury, another female recruit yelled out, "Ooooh, that looks expensive!" Yeah, they did not want to sweat out their hairdos and perms. But hey, would you rather get bust upside yo head with no protection?

We were also trained with police or security guard nightstick lookalikes. Again, some of us more knowledgeable recruits thought that they would be best if used like the baseball bats in the movie

Warriors. But there were rules to this shit. The instructors shouted "Move!" with every movement; the rear strike, the front strike, the comealong, the what-the-fuck strike. The nigga-you-must-be-crazy strike was most effective when corrections officers outnumbered the inmate or the inmate was shackled.

One day we took a break from class to go to lunch. We all filled our bellies and then fell asleep on the instructor for the second half of the day. Some recruits here were talking trash to one another about the class when one recruit took it to the extreme. He jokingly blurted out, "Shut the fuck up before I shove a plunger up your ass."

All of a sudden, dead silence. I mean crickets were squeaking. Even the instructor stood there in disbelief. *No, this muthafucka didn't! Oh, hell no!* It didn't help the situation that he was white and the one he shot the comment to was black. It didn't help that it was in the wake of the Abner Louima incident. And it didn't help that he was in arm's reach of me, either. No, no, no, no, no. None of these circumstances helped his ass at all. The instructor moved quickly after assessing the now-hostile situation and quickly escorted the inmate—I mean recruit—out of there! The next day, *BAM!* It was all in the papers. We never saw that recruit again and we received all sorts of training on what to say and how to act in the workplace.

You can't fail in the Academy unless you really do something drastic to get kicked out. Even if you fail a written test, they will let you take it again till you pass.

At the end of the Academy, right before we graduated, the instructor gave us a speech stating that basically the stuff that we were being taught was to cover their asses when we got inside the jails.

He told us that the real breakdown is that we are telling you how to do this shit. You ain't necessarily going to do it this way when you get inside the jails, but if you fuck up, don't say that we ain't teach you the right way to do it. These lessons are to cover our asses, not yours, when you fuck up.

All in all, some of the Academy was informative and some was pure bullshit. But ya boy graduated, and was now a bona fide corrections officer on his way to Rikers Island.

CHAPTER 9

NEW JACK CITY

"On the gate," a large CO yelled to another officer, who was inside the main control station, also known as gossip central.

The officer frowned and then turned the switch that opened the front gate. I was grateful to the other officer because this was my first day at my assigned jail and I had been standing at the gate for fifteen minutes to get in. *Here we go with the bullshit.* The jail I was assigned to was called C76, aka "the community center." As I walked in along with a slew of new officers, all we heard were comments from the senior officers.

"How many of these fuckin' jacks did we get?"

"There goes the fuckin' overtime."

One officer sniffed the air and said, "Aaah, you gotta love that fresh Academy smell." Another said, "Smells like shit to me. One of you muthafuckas lost your nerve already?" They all laughed. After roll call, I went to my assigned area and when I got there I said to myself, "Okay, big G, enough of the bullshit, get in there."

"Open the gate!" I yelled.

A small female CO came running to the gate, then stopped and said, "Shit, nigga, you yelling like you the police or something." Then she unlocked the gate and opened it just enough for me to brush up against her to get by. Now my heart was pumping. This is it, no more Academy scenarios, no more recruit shit. This is my debut as a corrections officer. I walk in to relieve the B officer, the secondary officer, and before I can formally introduce myself and take my mandatory count of the inmates, he tears the gate off its hinges getting the fuck out of there. The A officer, the primary, says to me, "Pick a side to go on, A or B." The housing area has two sides, which hold thirty to fifty inmates in each. I pick one. She opens the door to let me in, then slams it behind me. No conversation. I was warned about the bullshit senior officer/new officer rivalry. It didn't matter to me because, guess what, *I got the job, mootherrfuckerr!*

As soon as I got in there, I remembered how not impressed the inmates were when I made my first visit on OJT, on-the-job training. So I tried a different approach. I walked in quietly and took my count. In the Academy we learned that the count was the most important thing. This lets you, and the facility, know how many inmates are in your control at a time.

I was in a dormitory-like setting with beds lined up next to one another. I did as I was instructed to do in my Academy training. I proceeded to tap each sleeping inmate as I went by to observe if they moved or not, to make sure that they were still alive. All I heard from the startled inmates as I did this was "What the fu—!" Then, when they realized it was me, the CO, and not another inmate named big Smiddy trying to get some ass, they gave me the look like, "Oh, it's the CO." I'd heard that some officers who have been on the job awhile get comfortable and don't take mandatory counts when they assume a post. As a result, sometimes a dead inmate could go unnoticed for a long period of time. And the CO would have a lot of explaining to do.

"Ms. Jordan!" one inmate yelled out to the A officer.

"What!?" she responded.

"Could you call off your man Dudley Do-right. He walking around waking muthafuckas up," he yelled.

Then he glared at me and said, "Shit, nigga, tapping me like that while I'm sleeping could get your ass hurt!"

Then, before I could respond, the officer called me to the officers' station. She proceeded to scold me right in front of the inmates.

"Everything that you learned in the Academy, forget about it. It's a whole new ball game in here. So, sit down somewhere," she said.

Then she waved me off like she was busy, like I was in here just to start shit. She left me standing there looking stupid with all the inmates snickering and laughing at me.

Already I was bored to death. Outside these walls I may have seemed like this almighty corrections officer, but I was beginning to feel more like a glorified babysitter. *This can't be all there is to it with this job, just sitting here all day doing nothing.*

A few days go by and I'm slowly but surely getting the hang of this. I'm at another assigned post sitting down bored. *Some job.* The only fighting I'm doing is fighting sleep.

Then I hear someone say, "Gee?" *Uh-oh, that can only mean that this is someone who knows me from the streets.* I look and it's my man Biz. I knew that I would see people from the street but I did not think it would happen so soon. I instantly recalled that if I saw someone I knew I would have to put my foot down and enforce my status. Even if it was Biz, who my moms babysat when we were little and whose sister I used to smash out. This used to be my right-hand man back in the day. I had to let him know that I was a CO now and that he couldn't just be calling me Gee like that. How was I going to tell him this? I thought to myself, *Shit, nigga, this is your job now, your Michael Jordan sneakers for your kids, and someday your new house.*

Hell, this is your ghetto no-limit pass, your badge. I looked at him square in the face and said, "My name is Officer Heyward!" I told him that in here that is what he should call me and not to forget it. He stepped back in shock. He had the look like, "No this nigga didn't." He must have been thinking, *This nigga used to come to my house for sugar. I gave this lil nigga sneakers to wear to school—him and his brother. Wait until I call my moms and tell her that Gary Heyward from Public School 46, Miss Eldridge's class, is standing here fronting.* I know that he also thought that the real reason I seemed to be fronting was that I used to date his sister, and the word on the streets was that her head game was trash.

He slowly backed away and went and sat on his bed. I could see out of the corner of my eye that he was still in shock at how I acted and still staring at me. I knew that this was just the beginning. I wondered how many more times I would have to ignore my ghetto heritage, how many more times I would have to look my friends in the face and sell out my soul for the sake of my newfound livelihood. How many more times?

CHAPTER 10

REMINISCING

The day carried on and I was doing more stupid new jack shit like checking the doors and windows to make sure that they were locked and secure. I could see Biz out the corner of my eye watching me and figuring out a way to approach me. He finally came up to me the correct way, the way a friend who knows your history is supposed to approach you. A friend who knows that you're trying to hold down a job and do better for yourself. A friend who is not supposed to take it personal or blow your spot up when you act all professional and shit. He said, "Ah, CO, can I speak to you for a moment?" I said, "Yeah, what's up?" He apologized for approaching me the wrong way and we sat down and talked. We began to reminisce about our youth, from plastic coin food stamps—the black ones, fifty cents; the red, twenty-five cents—to drinking out of a fire hydrant on a hot summer day. That was before they started selling bottled water. Whoever thought of that is a fucking genius. He brought up the time when we were in several gangs, such as the G-force and Zulu Nation, and we got chased home by a rival gang called the Ball Busters. I remembered when we played this game on a chick named Tracy where we blindfolded her with a sock and placed different items in her hand. She was supposed to guess what they were. I put a frank in her hand

and she guessed frank. This nasty nigga Biz put his dick in her hand. You should have seen her squeezing and scrunching her face up trying to guess what it was. When she finally got it, she let out a yell and ran and told her mother. Talk about lil niggas getting their asses beat. Me and Biz ain't come outside for two summers. Yeah we were some crazy muthafuckas.

After we stopped laughing he said that he was going to let me know what was going on around here. Biz informed me that Rikers Island was a city inside the city. He told me that the COs here were making money, and he wasn't talking about their paychecks. He went on to say that some of his boys had gotten chick COs to bring them weed, razors, and all sorts of things. Some even gave up the pussy. I didn't believe him, because what I was told was that inmates lie on their dick all the time when it comes to fucking these female officers. I mean, it might have happened on a rare occasion, but the way that he was talking, it was like it was SOP (Standard Operating Procedure). He continued that he knew that a hustler like me was going to make a lot of money in here. I stared at him like he was crazy and said, "Ya see that's why I barked on you the way that I did earlier. Nigga, you of all people know where I come from. I ain't fucking my shit up for nothing." He said, "Gee, ain't no way that you can get caught, because you would be fucking with your right-hand man right here," pointing to himself. And there it was. I knew there was a reason for why he was giving me the rundown in this place, for the gas-me-up sales pitch. I ain't tear the nigga's head off right then. I just told him that I just got this job and that I wasn't fucking it up for nothing.

Convinced I was taking my job seriously, Biz moved on to a more moderate request. He said, "Look, Gee, I hear you and respect that." *The nigga's lying.* But he went on, saying, "On the real, a nigga is fucked up in here, so could you look out and hook me up with some cigarettes, not for me to smoke but so that I can juggle them."

"What the fuck is juggling?" I asked.

"Juggling is when the inmates trade the cigarettes between them for whatever, weed, food, and for phone calls (called clicks). Look around you, Gee," he pleaded, "everybody's smoking."

I did notice and I had just seen my A officer give her worker, an inmate, a cigarette a minute ago. *What am I going to do?*

I evaluated the situation. First, everybody was smoking. Second, they sold them in commissary, so it wasn't a crime for an inmate to have them. Third, the senior officers were giving them to the inmates anyway. Plus, I felt bad about barking on him this morning and this was my man Biz. I told him, okay, I'll hold him down this one time. He told me to go to his apartment, which was two floors down, and see his sister. And that she would give me a pack of cigarettes for him. Another reason I agreed to look out was that I had been seeing his sister around the hood and her ass had gotten fatter. She would often ask me when I was going to let her babysit my offspring again, meaning give me a blowjob. I definitely had to go check that out. I thought it was no big deal doing it, because it was only cigarettes.

CHAPTER 11

CORRECTION OFFICERS' BENEVOLENT ASSOCIATION

I had been on the job a few weeks. I was getting to know a lot of the officers and they were beginning to show me the ropes. I had already caught the eye of a few honeys that worked there and I had started to spit some game to them. *Getting my muthafuckin' mac on and shit.* One day while I was at lunch some old-timers snatched me up in the locker room and schooled me on how shit went around there—as far as pussy was concerned. One old-timer looked at me and laughed, then said, "Nigga, you having the time of yo life. Just look atcha, runnin' round here, up in all these bitches' faces telling ya corny jokes and shit. These dumb bitches justa laughin' and key keyin' at every little thang ya say. Ya gotcha hair all blown out and duddied up lookin' like a broke ass Steve Harvey and shit." Again he broke out into a loud hearty laugh. Of course this nigga was old, bald, and fat, so my thoughts were that he was just hatin' because it was my time to shine. So I just sat back and let Cooley High talk. He went on to say, "Looky here, yahoo, you ain't fuckin' funny. These bitches are just playing you like they play all these other Joe security fake-ass new niggas runnin' round here! They know you ain't have shit before ya got this job. They know how much ya make, how much ya bringing home after taxes and all that. Ya going round screaming that Harlem World shit!" He snickered. "They know you ain't got no car and ya probably still living witcha moms." He looked at me and saw that I was stuck. *How the fuck this nigga know all that?* He said, "Yeah, nigga, you're the new kid on the block, the new meat!" He laughed hard and loud. "Don't be fooled. None of these bitches are innocent. Let me guess, they just throwing da pussy atcha, huh?" he questioned. I nodded. The brother actually sounded a little upset over the whole issue. It was like he was talking to me but never seeming to be looking at me. He was always off into his own thoughts as if he was reminiscing about when he used to be me or something like that.

There were four or five elderly—I mean senior—officers changing their clothes. Some were bald, some with salt-and-pepper hair, some even had wooden teeth. Yes, wooden teeth, with all the benefits we get. There were others from the senior citizens corrections committee who overheard the officer, who looked like Rollo from *Sanford and Son*, talking to me and invited themselves into the conversation.

"Rufus, what are you doing talking to Baby Milk here? He ain't got enough time on the job to rate conversation," one of them said.

They laughed.

"Nah, I was just trying to let the youngun know how stupid he was looking around here and I was pointing him in the right direction," Rufus said.

Another officer said, "Like you know."

They laughed.

"Seriously, you can't be running around here like you never had pussy before. Believe me, you're gonna get your fair share of ass in due time, more than you can handle. Shit, everybody is fuckin' everybody! Officers, captains, deputies, everybody! Check it, you see all these female officers around here? A lot of them are loose with it. Even the bucktooth snooty bitches give up the ass on any given Sunday. Yeah, they all come in here the same way, like, 'I ain't fuckin' none of these niggas.'" He laughs, then he says, "I give them a three-month grace period before one of these officers has a finger in that pussy either on post or in the cocking lot—parking lot."

Another officer interjected, "Nah, all of them ain't that easy. It took me 'bout a year and a half to hit Officer Fredricks."

"You hit Fredricks?" Rufus asked with a stunned face.

The officer frowned and said, "That ass is old news, but it took me awhile."

"Ain't she married?" Rufus again questioned in disbelief.

The officer gave a da-fuck-wrong-witchu look and responded, "Yeah, and?" Then he turned to me and said, "Engaged, married, single, Baptist, Catholic, Muslim. It don't matter, 'cause if dey come up in here, dey fuckin'. Sometimes it's all about timing. Sometimes, if you work with them long enough the pussy just falls into your lap. Like I said, I was working with Fredricks for a minute before I popped her in the bathroom on overtime on the midnight tour. One night she came in to work drunk and upset about her husband leaving her because she worked too much. She went on to say that he felt that ever since she started this job it became her life. Everything is about the job, the parties, the niggas, everything! She said he had his shit packed when she left home to come to work. Yeah, that night she was in pretty bad shape and me being the loving and caring coworker that I am just sat there and listened, of course, after I went and got a fifth of Bacardi that I had in my stash."

They laughed and gathered around like all men do when we are about to hear some shit about a woman fucking that we want to fuck.

"I just sat there pouring her drink after drink, waiting patiently with my dick in my hand. Shit, after the captain made his tour and took a couple of shots to the head I knew it was on." He continued, "I had that ass hemmed up in that bathroom damn near all night! I ain't stop till they called the house out chow!"

They all burst out laughing. I sat there attentively listening, then another officer jumped in and said, "As soon as the chicks come through those gates from the Academy it's open season. It's a whole new world to these broads, because the Island is its own city and has its own rules. Watch, once you've been here awhile you going to be coming to work to hang out, drink, and fuck. This place is the ultimate getaway."

They laughed loud and hard.

"It's almost impossible to get caught cheating, especially if your chick ain't on the job," he said.

"What do you mean?" I asked.

"It's one way on and one way off Rikers Island and if you ain't no CO, then after visiting hours, you won't be able to come to a jail to check up on your spouse. And if they try and call, nine times out of ten, if you don't want to be found then you won't be found. You will be good to go once you get yourself a jail wife," he said.

"A jail wife?" I asked.

"Yeeeah, man," he said. "If you hook up with one of these shorties and y'all really feeling each other, she becomes your jail wife. She knows about your wife if you got one and you know about her man, but inside here y'all belong to each other. Everybody in the jail knows it and don't say shit at correction's officers functions when you show up with your real peoples. Shit, I done seen niggas leave their real wives for CO pussy."

"I done seen officers fight each other at roll call over dick and pussy that ain't even theirs, looking real stupid," Rufus chimed in.

"I saw an officer have a shootout in the parking lot after getting caught cheating. Of course his wife and mistress were both on the job. Shit, if them bitches get smart all they have to do is check ya pay stub to see if overtime is on it," another officer said.

"That ain't necessarily so," says another officer, "because I fucks them while they at work, straight time, overtime, it don't matter. There's so many offices and down-low spots in here, you can get a quickie in broad daylight if the broad is wit' it."

I give them a look like, "Y'all crazy." One of them yells from the row of lockers next to us and says, "If somebody is married to one of these COs in here, they know when their shit gets shaky at home. They know when their people's normal movements have changed. They know when they start acting different because of this job. They know when COBA (Correction Officers' Benevolent Association) done turn they lil asses out!" Everybody laughs.

CHAPTER 12

BITCH ASS NIGGAS

After the officers finished getting dressed and left, I sat there in the dirty locker room soaking up all the stuff I'd just heard. I looked around and noticed that I was sitting in the cemetery, a row of beat-up lockers that were sealed with tape, with the words "Rest in Peace" written on them. Later I found out that when officers pass away on the job, their lockers are taped up with all their belongings inside. To me it was a bullshit jailhouse ritual, because I also heard about officers acting like scavengers and breaking into these so-called sacred lockers and stealing their contents. I'm sure there were a bunch of officers walking around with dead men's uniforms and no guilt whatsoever.

I was about to leave when another officer came into the row where I was sitting. He asked if he could sit down and talk to me. He was a tall man with a slender build and a bald head. Well, I thought he was bald until I noticed that he had one long braid attached to the back of his head. It looked like the barber shaved everything but that one braid. *Somebody needs to beat that barber's ass.* He sat down and began to talk.

"I overheard y'all's conversation," he said.

Then he looked at me with a raised eyebrow and said, "Yo, don't listen to those muthafuckas. A lot of them niggas are bruised, bitter, and just plain ol' beat up. Sure, they will sit here and talk all the shit in the world about the females around here, but nothing about their trifling asses. A lot of them just walk around here mad because they fucked their lives up. You see, Rufus," he said, "he's what you a call a BAN."

"What's that"? I asked.

"A bitch ass nigga. The type of CO that never was nobody before this job, got bullied in high school, and never got no chicks. You know, the type of nigga who always wound up sitting in the living room or in the car while you're in the room fuckin'. The muthafucka never could fight until he took up martial arts, and now he comes on this job to get vengeance on all these cuffed dudes in here who remind him of who and what he really is deep down. Then you have Kev," he went on, not realizing that I didn't know these guys by their first names. "He is what you call an SAN."

"What's that?" I asked.

"A stupid ass nigga. He diddybopping around here still trying to live out his heyday. The nigga damn near fifty and he's still dyeing his hair, buying gold chains and rings and shit. Muthafucka been on the job over ten years and don't own nothing, no property, no bonds, no CDs, nothing. He just buys mink coats and gator shoes and hits every CO party, hemming up these new naive broads that come through here. The nigga ain't even smart enough to go to the dentist. All this nigga's teeth are just rotten and missing on one side. He can only chew on the left side of his mouth."

We both laughed out loud.

"Watch 'im the next time he's trying to eat a piece of rib or something. It's like torture to his ass! Chris and Paul are FANs."

I asked his ass what that was.

"They're faggot ass niggas. These red, white, and blue bleeding muthafuckas will do anything for this job. This job is their life! If you ever looking for them, you will find them standing on top of Corrections Mountain with the CO flag wrapped around them blowing in the wind. Do me a favor and don't ever talk disrespectfully about this job to those George Washingtons, because they will be ready to fight. This job is their reason for living. Everything they do revolves around this job in one way or another. This piece of dirt we standing on is their reason for living. They go to every CO party, every cookout, every sports event and all dat. They give their kids names after the jails like Rosy for Rose M. Singer and Benny for the Bing and all dat. The shit is crazy, man," he said, chuckling to himself. "To them, in their world, if you ain't a CO you're an inmate, point-blank."

Then he looked at me and said, "All of them muthafuckas got caught up in here chasing pussy. How do you think that they can tell you all so well about what's going to happen to you? It's because they have been through it and still going through it. Divorce and child support ruined them. They can't get through the day without a drink and a lot of times they take their frustrations out on these inmates because they have the power to do so. All because they wanted to fuck everything that moved up in this bitch." He paused, and then said, "Just like you."

As he got up to leave he said, "Tell me something."

I gave him a look like, "What?"

"Which one are you going to be?" he asked me while walking out.

CHAPTER 13

GUNSHOTS

I had made my way to the COs' kitchen after being schooled in the locker room when I heard CO Spiff yell "Johnson! Johnson!" in the face of an inmate that was on the serving line in the officers' kitchen.

"What!" yelled CO Johnson from the back of the kitchen.

CO Johnson walked out to the front to confront CO Spiff.

"Tell this stupid inmate to give me two pieces of chicken!" yelled CO Spiff at the top of his lungs.

Spiff stood there with a large Tupperware bowl he had brought from home. No orange serving tray for him. I wondered to myself, *How is it that we go to these inmates' cells or dorms where they sleep and toss their belongings all on the floor, rip up their pictures from home, and sometimes unnecessarily destroy sacred personal items during our random searches, then expect those same inmates not to piss or spit or worse, bust a nut in the food that they serve us?* Most of the time the kitchen staff are unsupervised. So they can easily plan and execute revenge in their own little way if they really wanted to.

CO Johnson ordered the inmate to give CO Spiffy Spiff another piece of chicken (Spiffy Spiff is what he had marked on his inmate-issue green cup). Spiff reached over and took the inmate's identification card off his shirt. He put it in his pocket, knowing that every officer the inmate encountered for the remainder of the day would give him hell for not having his ID card. *Stupid shit.*

I got my food and began to think about all the things that had been said in the locker room while watching all the other officers around me. Some were asleep, some were watching television, and a couple of female officers were bringing male officers lunch. I learned that that's the first telltale sign that they're fucking. I laughed to myself, because in here trying to be low-key is impossible. Then I heard a typical CO conversation from a table full of officers who reeked of liquor and cigarettes.

"So the mate kept talking shit, going on about how he was going to fuck my mother when he got out, how he was going to have my sister sucking dick for a living and all dat!" said one male CO to a female CO.

Her response was sucking her teeth and saying, "Sheeeiit!"

She was making a face like no way the inmate would say that to her.

"I just let him talk. I didn't say a word. Since we were in the intake area, I just processed him and let him go to court," the male CO said. "Then about six that night, that muthafucka came back from court and I was waiting. I hurried up and processed all the other inmates and left his black ass for last." The female was now in his face drooling. He had her full undivided attention, like she got off on these stories.

"After everybody was gone, I had Officer Smith handcuff the mate to the bars of the cell. You should have heard that nigga complaining. 'What is this? I'm tired. I just came from court! Why am I still here?' Then his face turned pale white when he saw me walk into that cell and lock it behind me. You should have seen him squirming, trying to get loose from them cuffs! He was a big nigga, too. I slowly put on my straightliners, you know, my black leather gloves with the metal inserts. Then I proceeded to whip his ass! Piyow, right to his jaw! I repeated to him all the shit that he said to me that morning with every punch. 'Piyow, you're gonna fuck my moms, right? Pow, that's for my sister. You remember her, right?"

The female officer looked like she was fingering herself because she was so excited with what he was saying. The officer continued, "When I finished with him, they rushed his ass out of there pronto right to Elmhurst Hospital." Back then officers didn't have to worry about all the lawsuits and bullshit that are going on now.

The female officer responded, "Shit, fuck them mates. If their families are so worried about their loved ones, they should make sure they don't come to jail. Period." They laughed.

Then all of a sudden, *BLLIIINNGLIINNG!* A loud bell started sounding off. It was an alarm. This was my first one and I was stunned. I saw officers scrambling to put their food away. Some just left theirs right there. Some females with expensive hairstyles ran toward the bathroom to hide, while the rest of us burst into action. The alarm meant that some officer was in trouble, probably getting their ass kicked or about to be kicked. We had to hurry up and get down there, because we all knew that the ratio of inmate to officer was on the inmate side when things first jumped off. We knew that the officer, male or female, had to fend for themselves until help arrived.

At first I never understood why there was only one officer per fifty inmates and how the system we ran allowed us to maintain control. I learned that an officer on the floor or patrolling the area where the inmates were is the sacrificial lamb, and the officer behind the protective bars or glass is the one that is being counted on to notify the supervisor of what's happening to the lamb—I mean other officer.

I rushed to the staging area, my heart pumping like crazy, my adrenaline flowing, along with a shitload of nervousness. *This is it, big boy. Don't get your ass beat up on your first alarm.* I made it to the staging area in a hurry, only to be told by a captain to slow down and properly put on all the protective equipment that we are supposed to wear when we go into battle. I was stunned, because an officer could have been getting killed down there and this supervisor was worried about whether I was putting on shin guards to protect my legs. I looked over to another officer to see if he was just as disturbed as I was, and he said, "Ya better put on everything, because if you go down there and get seriously hurt and it's because you did not have on the proper equipment, Corrections insurance is not going to cover you." *Oh, shit!* Then I yelled to the fat officer that was conveniently stuck with passing out the equipment, "Give me a muthafuckin' shin guard." After putting on all the proper stuff, I ran down to the area with the first wave.

We arrived at the area where the alarm was sounding and saw inmates yelling and begging to be let out of the housing area. The captain ordered them to back up so that he could locate the officers. Precaution was taken because we did not see the officers at first and this could have been a hostage situation. Then the officers appeared and they were just as frantic as the inmates were to get out of there. We unlocked the gate and the inmates all fled out, quickly hitting the floor with their hands behind their heads, letting us know that they were not a threat. Then the officers approached the captain and one of them, a female, said, "Ga-ga-gunshots!" Then she burst into tears and repeated, "I heard gunshots!"

Have you ever seen the cartoon where there are a bunch of people in line and the first person stops, then the rest bump into him? Well, that was me bumping into the captain as he made a sudden stop. *Oh, heeeell no! Benefits don't cover this shit here. These riot suits are not bulletproof.* I looked at the captain like, "These muthafuckas are shooting and you're worried about shin guards?"

We stood there dumbfounded, all of us looking at the captain for our next move. He hesitated, then took a deep breath and told us that we had to go in. We looked at one another, then we followed our fearful leader.

We edged our way forward. Nobody wanted to be the first one inside. I was right next to the captain. Okay, okay, I was right behind the captain. We entered and saw one lone inmate lying on his back on his bed screaming that he had been shot. Of course we were all hoping that he was lying. But as we got closer we saw that he wasn't. He had a gunshot wound to his leg. *Oh, shit!* The evidence was right there. Somehow an inmate had been able to get a gun inside this jail. I couldn't believe it. I was working in this very housing area just a few days before and talking shit to these inmates like I was invincible, never thinking that one of these individuals had a firearm in his possession. A whirlwind of questions hit me all at once: How did he get it? Which one of them had it? Who shot the gun? And, most important, where was the weapon right now? Does one of the inmates that we let out have it? Did we just put the whole jail in danger by not assessing the situation correctly?

I could tell that all of us were thinking the same thing. The captain went over to the inmate and asked him, "Where is the gun?" The inmate stated that he did not know. He said that somebody just shot him for nothing. The captain, now with composure regained but still realizing that we were not out of hot water, belted out orders. "Search those inmates out there! The weapon is still missing." He continued, "Officers, spread out and search every inch of this place. I want it turned upside down. I want that weapon found."

Over the radio I heard the deputy warden on duty calling the captain to see what the situation was. *This ought to be good.* He stuttered and said, "Si . . . sir, it would appear that an inmate has been shot." We all heard the radio drop, then a loud "WHAT?" The captain said, "Yes, sir, you heard me correctly, an inmate appears to have a single gunshot wound to his thigh." The next transmission was "I am sending the second and third waves in."

They arrived and aided us with tearing the place apart. Then a female officer overturned a locker and gasped. When we came over to see what she had found, we were all stunned to see a .22-caliber gun lying on the floor. All of us new jacks looked like, "What the fuck is going on in here?" The senior officers all had a look that said they had been here before.

"Nobody touch it!" the captain yelled.

All the jail's heavy hitters were now on deck. All sorts of chiefs and wardens and Investigation Department representatives were swarming in, each trying to look more important than the next. The rest of the day was total chaos. Who's at fault? Did the officers do their job right? Whose head is going to roll? And so on. All I could think about was what the Academy taught us about officers bringing in things for inmates. I remembered the instructor saying, "If an officer will bring in a stick of bubblegum for an inmate, he will bring in a gun." Those words kept ringing in my head. I wondered, could an officer really be capable of bringing in a gun for an inmate to use?

Let's take a quiz, shall we?

An inmate is being supervised at all times by who? A CO.

An inmate has to be thoroughly searched when he comes into the building by who? A CO.

An inmate has to pass through metal detectors to get inside the jail and the detectors are manned by who? A CO.

An inmate has to be searched again before entering and leaving the housing area by who? A CO.

Final question: What mode of transport can bypass all these preventive measures and can circumvent all the COs who are placed in various security positions throughout the jail? The answer: a CO!

CHAPTER 14

STOOL PIGEON

For the next couple of days things were on lockdown on some fake ass tight security and shit. All of a sudden, we were now doing our jobs the way we were supposed to be. We were enforcing the most trivial institutional rules. Where's your ID? Clear the magnometer! A *beep-beep* from the machine indicating that the inmate had metal on him somewhere and you heard, "Strip! Take everything off and go through again!" Yeah, we were giving the inmates hell. A tactical search operation or TSO was in full effect. We had officers from the other jails visit and help search the place. Sometimes this was done to shake the inmates up, just to let them know that there were consequences to them acting up.

After the hoopla died down I was assigned again to the same housing area as Biz. I was sitting in a chair in the dorm area where inmates were watching TV.

"What did I tell you?" he said.

"What?" I asked.

"You know that an officer brought in that gun, right?"

"Yeah, right?"

"I'm serious," he said. "Some of us knew it was going to go down before it happened."

I just looked at him. I knew he was dead serious.

"I know whoever did it got paid, because the inmate is going to sue the shit out of Corrections," he said.

I sat there listening to him and thinking, *Damn, here I am bringing him cigarettes, feeling guilty and shit, and other officers are bringing in artillery!* I shook my head at the thought, then I said to Biz, "By the way, your sister called me and said that you wanted some more cigarettes."

He smiled and said, "Yo, tell her I'm good. In fact, tell her I am good for the next three maybe four months." Puzzled, I asked, "How is that? Just a minute ago your lungs were on the gate and you needed help and now you're sitting here like you're big OG and you run the joint." He laughed and said, "That's because I do, thanks to you." I gave him the "huh?" face. He broke it down to me.

"Ya see, those little packs of cigarettes that you bought me?" he said.

"Yeah?" I asked.

"Well, I had my sister put a little somethin' inside them to help my cause," he said.

"What?" I asked, a little too loudly, and he motioned for me to keep it down so the other inmates could not hear. "Like what?"

"She put a little weed in the packs and sealed them back up," he admitted.

I was getting pissed. We just stared at each other for what seemed like an eternity. *This nigga played me.* He could see the anger begin to grow, and before I could say anything he gave me a pleading look like, "Remember where we're at." I took heed his gesture and slowly calmed down. "Come on, Gee," he said, "it wasn't even a lot. It was just enough for me to get on my feet."

I sat there knowing that the only words that would come out my mouth if I did speak would be "Hee haw! Hee haw!"

"You ain't gonna blow a nigga up, are you?" he pleaded again. "Check it, you helped my family because you know they ain't got no money to be sending me for commissary every two weeks." He paused and looked at me thankfully. "Now they don't have to worry about me for a while."

I just looked at him, trying to convince myself that we weren't once close friends. As if I did not have to look at our families' faces damn near every day. Just the other day his moms and my moms stood in the lobby of our building and talked for hours. I went past them and his moms asked me how he was doing.

I considered beating Biz's ass. But how could I? He was right about one thing: We are at my job and I am an officer and that means that not only can I not blow him up, I can't blow myself up either. I shook my head, thinking that this was supposed to be a friend of mine and he used me. Just imagine if it was some smooth-talking hustling individual from the streets that conned me into doing this? If so, I would be fucked. I would really be at the inmate's mercy. Thank God it was Biz or I would have put myself in a position to be pimped every muthafuckin' day when I came to work.

That was it for me. From that point on, it was "Don't trust no fuckin' inmate for shit! They gets nothing from me, not a goddamn thing." That's right, I transformed back to "scared nigga" mode.

Just as I was finished with Biz the captain walked into the area and motioned for me to step outside with him. Then he handed me a piece of paper and said, "Take care of yourself." Then he walked away. I looked at the paper. It stated that I was transferred to another jail. No formalities or I am sorry to see you go, just get the fuck out.

I was just beginning to get adjusted but I was told that because I was new, a transfer was a possibility. C-76, the jail I was working now, was an alright jail and kind of laid-back, nothing like the stories that I've heard about the other jails on the Island. I stood there with this feeling of not knowing what was going to happen next. That was when the bubbleguts in my stomach started acting up and I ran to the bathroom.

CHAPTER 15

WELCOME TO THE NEIGHBORHOOD

"CO, CO!" an inmate yelled out to me.

I had just taken over post 2 top at the new jail, C-73. I was a little nervous, because when I got there and reported to Personnel, there were no formalities at all. The officer who handled my paperwork did not even look up to see my face or acknowledge me. He just asked me my name and then gave me my post assignment. Then he yelled out, "Next!" I felt like I was just thrown in there. No debriefing to let me know how to do anything on my new post. Nothing. I was just handed the keys and rushed to sign a count slip that I was supposed to verify. This is important, because your count is supposed to match the count of the officer that you're relieving. If the count doesn't match that means that there is an inmate missing and you're not supposed to sign the count slip. If you sign the count slip you're acknowledging that all the inmates are accounted for and now you're liable if one them is missing. So, here I am trying to get my bearings and I am now hearing several inmates yell, "CO! CO!"

I stood up and looked down a long tier that consisted of

thirty-one cells. I see smoke coming from under one of the inmate's doors and realize that an inmate has set his cell on fire. *Oh, shit, this is the real deal!* I remember other COs telling me that C-76, the jail that I came from, was nothing but a community center compared to this jail. I continued to brainstorm. *Okay, muthafucka, this is what you signed on for, so what are you going to do first?* Now, here come all the Academy nightmares. It could be a setup. The inmates could be using the fire as a diversion just to get me down there so they could jump me. Should I open his cell? Do I call the Fire Department? Do I call my area supervisor? All this shit is happening too fast. I had to think fast. If I call my supervisor, by the time he gets here, the inmate could be burned to a crisp. *Fuck it.* I call for my area supervisor. I was not running down there playing superhero.

My conscience begins to talk to me: *But ain't that your job? Care, custody, and control of these inmates, remember? To hell with that shit. Fuck with me, they're going to be sweeping up his ashes! I can always rely on being STD (Scared to Death).*

The captain arrived on my gate and I opened it and told him in a hyped tone that an inmate set his cell on fire. I was letting him know that there was a sense of urgency to handle the situation. He strolled in at a snail's pace, looked at me like, "You fucking jack" and then calmly walked down to the inmate's cell. When he got in front of the inmate's cell I was right behind him with a fire extinguisher. He waved for me to stop and not to come any closer. So I stopped and stood there with the smoke coming from under the door. The captain proceeded to have a conversation with the inmate.

"You're pulling this bullshit now at the end of my fucking tour!" he said.

The inmate spoke but I could not hear him, but I did hear another inmate from another cell say, "Ain't nobody fucking with him, Cap."

"So you're telling me that you waited till now to tell me that you're having problems in this house and that you can't live here?" the captain said sarcastically.

The inmate responded again in a low voice, in between coughing. Again, I could not hear. Then the captain motioned for me to come closer and I did. Then he grabbed the fire extinguisher from me without the inmate knowing. He turned his face toward me and mouthed for me to go and crack open the inmate's cell. I did as I was told. When the door was cracked, the captain let loose, spraying the inmate's face. Then he kicked him to the floor inside the cell and continued putting out the fire, at the same time making sure the inmate got a mouthful. My dumb ass just stood there looking stupid. He soaked the inmate's clothes, his bed, and anything he could reach with the extinguisher.

"Muthafucka, you ain't going nowhere!" he yelled. "You got problems in here? Huh, huh? Deal with them. Ya shouldn't have brung yo ass to jail."

Then he dragged the inmate out of his cell and slammed him up against the wall outside his cell. I heard and saw the inmate's head bounce off the wall. The inmate grabbed the back of his head as he slid to the ground and I could see blood begin to spew from his injury. *Oh, shit! What the fuck am I supposed to do now? Am I in some sort of trouble? Is the inmate going to claim that I was in on this assault? Am I going to have to write reports on what just happened? If I do, do I snitch on the captain or do I lie about what happened so that we don't get into trouble?*

I stood there pondering my next move. The captain knelt next to the now-semiconscious inmate and asked him if he needed medical attention. It was a rhetorical question, because the captain had this look on his face like, "Ya better not." The captain then asked, "What happened to your head?" The inmate responded that he had slipped and fallen when he came out of the shower. The captain patted him softly on his face and said, "Okay then, you'll be alright." He then stood up and calmly walked by me toward the exit and, sensing that my eyes were on him, without turning around, said, "Welcome to the neighborhood."

CHAPTER 16

THE STOOL SOFTENER

"Big Hey-woooood!"

My name is being shouted out by a fellow officer when I enter the jail on my way to roll call.

"Yooooooooo! What's poppin'? What's poppin'?" I respond.

"I saw you last night at the party, nigga. Did you hit?" he asks.

I give him a look of disappointment because I notice that the other male officers, who are standing in the lineup against the wall, all stopped talking to hear my answer. I sarcastically say to him, "Yo, who does that?" He gives me a puzzled look like he doesn't understand the question. I say loudly, "I mean, really, who's the only kid you know that not only tells his boys what females he's going to hit, but also gives you the time and date of when it's going down? Huh? Huh?" I ask him. "I CAN'T HEAR YOU!" I sing out.

They laugh.

"I told y'all he was going to front. This nigga ain't hit," he says to the other officers.

I shake my head calmly and say, "Another nonbeliever." Then I say, "Bet I did."

"Whooooooo?" everybody croons on this high school shit.

"Bet a buck," he says.

"Ya know he's still a jack; that might be a little too steep for him," another officer says.

"Bet," I say.

Then he pulls out a hundred-dollar bill. Looking at the rest of the fellas, he asks out loud, "What you do, bring in ya momma's panties or something as proof?" They laugh. I step up to all of them as they quiet down and pull out my cell phone (yeah, the one we are not supposed to have inside the jail). As they look at me, I'm busy into my phone scrolling down pressing buttons whistling to myself. Then I calmly gesture for the group of tenth-grade, pathological, non-pussy-getting liars to come closer. Excluding the officer who bet me, I proceed to show them some pictures I took the previous night.

"Daaammmmn!" they all respond simultaneously.

The nonbelieving officer grabs my phone so he can get a closer look for verification. He looks at the picture I have of the female officer in question, on her knees with my dick in her mouth.

"How I know that that's you? I don't see your face nowhere on that picture," he says, making a last-ditch effort not to pay up.

The others give me a look like he's right, siding with his frivolous attempt to avoid paying me.

"I knew that you were going to say that," I say while taking my phone back from him.

Then I push the button on my phone to move to the next picture and show him and only him the shot.

"Daaaaamn!" he shouts out.

Then he gives me my phone and my money and starts bowing down like I am a king or something. They all rush to see what he saw on my phone. They burst out laughing when they see that I took a picture in the mirror of me hitting her from the back in the bathroom.

Yeeeeeah, man, time has blown by and I've become that bitch ass/ faggot ass/stupid ass CO that the officers from the locker room were talking about. I mean I jumped right into the swing of things, from the parties, the basketball team, the going to Joey's (a local bar where a lot of COs hang out) to the drinking on post, and the shitting on inmates every chance I got (thanks to Biz playing me). All the inmates I shat on should have said, "Thank you, Biz!" Yessir! Yessir! I am a full-fledged backstabbing, pussy-tapping, robbing-the-City-by-going-to-sleep-on-the-midnight-tour CO. Even though I still live with my moms, I have stepped my game up immensely. I've bought a green Dodge Caravan from Major World Auto—where everybody goes with fucked-up credit. Don't act like it's just me. I no longer have just one pair of black pants to go partying in. I now have two pair, one of them leather. I bought my first pair of gators and all dat. Yeah, baby, I'm ballin'! I am a crowd favorite when it comes to snapping and joking around the jail. And guess what? These fools done fucked around and let a nigga purchase a firearm. It's a gat, a ratchet, a biscuit, a burner, an ooowhhop to anybody over fifty. Ha, ha, I am on top of the wooorrrld!

Mental note: Negro ain't say shit about taking his kids anywhere, spending time with them, or buying them anything. Well, I guess I can always blame it on all the overtime I am doing. Yeah, that's it . . . overtime.

The white shirts (these are captains or above) come down the hall to address us at roll call. We all stand in line formation on some paramilitary shit for morning inspection. We are required to have a memo book that we keep our daily activities logged in, a 911 knife, which is a switchblade that curves, used when an officer on the midnight tour wakes up to find an inmate dangling from a suicide attempt inside his or her cell, a flashlight, and OC spray, which is a form of pepper spray.

While we were being inspected, two officers from our security department roll out a wooden cabinet with two doors on it. They position it in front of our line, upright, so that everyone can see its contents. Then they open the doors and reveal to us all sorts of weapons that they have confiscated from inmates at some time in the past. They had all kinds of shanks in there produced by innovative inmates. One captain starts to point to some of them and tells us where they were found.

"This one was found under the radiator, this one on top of a light fixture," he said.

It was a sharpened piece of plastic. He stated that the inmates got smart and started using them to pass through the metal detectors. With a serious look on his face, holding up the plastic shank wrapped in rubber bands, he continued, "This can and will go right through that stab-proof vest that y'all be wearing if the right amount of force is applied. This one's my favorite," he says, taking a seven-inch sharpened pipe out of the display case. "I call it the stool softener because it was removed from an inmate's anus."

All of us relatively new officers looked on in shock. A senior officer belted out, "Goddamn, Cap, how many times are you going to show us these old shits?" The captain gives a look like, "Okay smartass" and then says, "You're right, CO Chase, so now let's take a look at some other items that we found on inmates recently."

He then pulls out a small box from the bottom of the display case. Then he takes out of the box some Gemstar razors and about fifteen surgical scaffolds. We all stand there stunned. Then the captain says, "And these are no makeshift bangers or shanks. Sheeeit, some of them still have the price tag on them from the store." He looks at big-mouth Chase and says, "Maybe we need to dust them for your fingerprints."

Chase responds, "Stop playing, Cap, that ain't funny."

"No, it ain't funny," the captain says while walking down the formation with the items held up in his hands. He says, "These items were not made up by inmates, these items were brought in here"— he pauses to let his words sink in, then continues—"either by way of counselor, or inmate visitor, or, ultimately, an officer."

Dead silence. No one said a word.

He continues, announcing some more good news, stating that our fearless mayor has decided to add to our already dangerous and tough job by putting into law a no-smoking rule for all city-owned buildings.

The complaining starts.

"That's bullshit," officers complain. "That don't include us, right, Cap? He always starting some shit and we got to clean it up."

"Calm down, calm down," the captain said.

Everybody got quiet so he could speak. "We still have a job to do. We still have to maintain care, custody, and control of these inmates." Then he dismisses us and we look at each other for a moment, letting all the risk sink in, understanding the new law will trigger tension with the inmates. Then, simultaneously, we hit him again with a barrage of complaints and questions.

"Why we always gotta get hit with the bullshit?" "What's going to happen with these inmates that have been smoking all their lives?" "Is the mayor bringing his ass down here to help us out?"

Officer Swartz, who always has a sick sense of humor, blurts out, "Go on now, go on now. Y'all keep yo trap shut and do what y'all's told. Now git! Ya hear me? Git back to them fields and get massa's cotton."

CHAPTER 17

CARE. CUSTODY. CONTROL.

Every officer has to adhere to the three Cs. I'll break it down for you, Big Heyward style.

Care: Officers must tend to all the inmates' needs, such as feeding them, getting them their medication, and occasionally, if the officer feels generous, allowing them to take a decent shit by giving them toilet paper.

Custody: Officers must escort the inmates wherever they need to go, by getting up from their comfortable seats to lock and unlock gates and cells, handcuffing and shackling them for various reasons, and occasionally, if the officer feels generous, allowing them the option every hour on the hour to go into their cells for various reasons. Tah! Try that shit for eight hours, talking about a muthafucka running back and forth.

And last but not least, control: Officers must maintain control by making sure their inmate count is correct, by checking inmates' passes as they walk the hall so that, for example, inmate Abdul from area 1 main cannot sneak around the jail to go to area Sprung 4 to see his man Ice. This helps prevent the occasional juggling of goods, gang communication, such as kites (a written request from one inmate to another), and inmate assaults, such as face cuts or stabbings. And if the officer is generous, he or she maintains control by issuing an occasional ass-whipping.

And then there's the fourth C (although not an official C), which is the consoling officers do by listening to an inmate talk about his case, his family, and how he's either going to beat a murder charge in trial or finish his sentence when the sun burns out.

I can't forget about the arguing either—yes, the arguing with your spouse over the phone about why you ain't home, how come you had to do overtime again. I know many officers have heard this: The officer: "Why aren't you answering your phone at night when I call you from work where you know that I can't just leave and go find your ass?" And the significant other's response is: "Why you always wait till the last minute to say you're working overtime and when I call the jail they can't find you and you know that there is no way that I can come over there and find yo black aaassss?"

Not to mention the officer can't pick up the kids from the babysitter, missed another birthday, another holiday.

Officers must deal with all these things and so much more. Yeah, this job comes with a lot of stress.

Roll call is over and we are dismissed. I leave and do what any red-blooded CO would do who knows his anxious and deserving co-workers are waiting to be relieved of duty. I run my ass to the staff kitchen. Yeah, baby. You know, I need to talk some more shit to that dude who thought that I did not hit.

I enter the staff kitchen and the usual is going on. One officer is over by the serving station asking an inmate for more grits on his plate and the inmate is just smiling while giving her an extra scoop. I shake my head. Another officer is yelling, "Goddamnit! Somebody ate my food that I brought from home out of the refrigerator." A fat officer nearby is just sitting there whistling while cleaning out his fingernails. I chuckle. Then I see my three favorite officers, Bryant, K. Johnson, and Z. Jones. These three female officers, along with a few inmates whom I have gotten to know, were responsible for everything that I knew at this job up to this point. So I go over to sit down and chat with them.

Note: The officers awaiting relief were supposed to be on their way home by 7:30 p.m. By the time that I sit my black ass down with the three officers it's 7:28 p.m. So the waiting officers were now either a) calling the control room to see if I came to work; b) waiting impatiently in the hallway for me to enter my post; or c) keeping it gangsta and coming down to the staff kitchen to meet me, leaving their inmates unguarded and handing me the keys to my post.

YEAH, I'M A PIECE OF SHIT!

Then, all of a sudden, *BLLIIINNG! BLIIIING!* A muthafuckin' alarm. I get up and run for the door, passing the smiling inmate staff kitchen workers. They're smiling because they know that the officers who had food from home or the store have to leave it right there for them to clean up. To them, someone's half-eaten fast food from outside is like hitting the Lotto.

I'm running toward the staging area, where we put our protective equipment, when the captain yells, "Ten-thirteen! Come with me now, there's no time for that." He means that an officer is in need of immediate assistance. Four other burly officers and I run down the corridor toward the area where the officer is being assaulted. As we're running, I hear hard breathing and panting from the officers and I smell last night's drinking on all of us. I have a flashback about my training. I recall the lesson about how to control my breathing when running, how to not let the excitement and adrenaline control my actions, and how to assess the situation in seconds and take the best course of action. Most of all, I remember to pace myself, because getting tired is not an option while running into battle. That training didn't come from the Corrections Academy; it came from my being the true marine that I am on the inside and will always be (Semper Fi).

We are a few yards away from the area when we see two officers struggling with an inmate. There are one female and one male and both of them are relatively small. The inmate is really giving them a tough time and the female officer has pulled his hoodie over his face so he cannot see. As we get closer we notice that her nose is bleeding. That is it! If there is anything that will send the pack into a frenzy it is the opportunity to avenge a damsel in distress. We converge on the inmate like an army of ants on the Discovery Channel. I strike first and hear a loud thud when I land a hard left to his ribs. The female officer then falls back into "I am a woman and he hit me" mode. Then the other officers and I begin to pound and stomp the inmate. Our attack is so fierce that I feel the wind on my face from the blows the other officers are giving him. The inmate is now down on the ground in a fetal position trying to fight back. The stomping continues and he is receiving scuff marks from Timberland, Mountain Gear, Bates, and Skechers. *Who the fuck was wearing Skechers?* As the rest of the probe team arrives to join in on the onslaught, I back up to take a breather, and that's when the inmate's hood comes off and I can see the damage that I have done to his face.

My heart sinks and my whole body goes numb. I stand there as the officers continue to stomp on him. It is like I am watching it in slow motion. I see a boot repeatedly come down on the left side of his face and the delayed reaction of the right side of his face hitting the floor. Blood spews everywhere. That is when my eyes and the inmate's eyes lock. He looks at me and just stops fighting back, even though the officers continue the "rehabilitation process." I don't know what to do next. My mouth opens but no words come out and I can't move. The inmate just stares at me with this I-can't-believe-this-shit-is-happening expression on his face. I want to say something. I want to do something. I want anything to happen that would make them stop. Instead, I do nothing. I ask myself, "What am I supposed to do, jeopardize my job?" I mean, how would it look if I jumped in there on this inmate's behalf and pushed and shoved officers, telling them to stop this excessive beating? I know what would happen if I did that. I would be crucified throughout my entire career, that's what. My mind, my heart, my soul say that this is wrong and that I should do something. Yet I still stand there with my eyes about to tear up knowing, deep down, that I have started this and that they are finishing it. I do nothing to help this person, this human being, this inmate. I do nothing to help my friend. I just stand there and watch them fuck Biz up.

CHAPTER 18

GOD, HUH?

After target practice was over, the captain told me and the other officers who first arrived on the scene to leave and that the probe team would fill out the incident reports. This way we would not be named in what just happened. As we walked away down the corridor, senior officers were patting me on the back and applauding the ass-beating. It was like now they could trust me. I was official. I had proven myself. I was one of them. Word had traveled throughout the jail that Big Heyward had put that work in. I was getting nods of approval from male officers and stares from some female officers. Later that day bits and pieces of information about the incident began to surface. I'd heard that the female officer got into it with Biz because he didn't have an ID card and that he didn't assault the female officer after all. It turns out that she just gets nosebleeds every time she gets excited.

I knew the other officers didn't really care whether Biz deserved the ass-whipping or not. All they knew about the incident was that an inmate had fought back and busted a female officer's nose. And any inmate who does stuff like this is going to be made an example of so that when word gets around the jail, the other inmates will think twice before pulling such a stunt.

Hearing about what led up to the incident made me feel worse, because I was still feeling like shit and wondering how I was going to explain this to Biz's mother once she heard about what I'd done, and to the people in my neighborhood who found out. What would be the consequences of my actions? The fact that I, along with my coworkers, had just violated an inmate's rights didn't worry me. I knew that that would be handled in-house. Nor was I worried about how Biz was going to answer the questions from the hospital staff about how this happened. Biz had been in and out of the system for a while, so he knows the "I slipped and fell in the shower" routine. What had me worried was what was going to happen when he got out or when he recovered and called home to the hood to tell them what I did. Word would spread faster than a crack dealer giving out free samples. For a CO, it's always a risk to run into inmates that you know. Now I had beef with one of them who happens to live in my building and knows my whole circle of friends. This is why COs move out of the hood, to avoid an encounter with a former inmate. I would've moved out, too, if I had had more money saved. Now I wanted to move more than ever.

When I arrived at the staff kitchen to have lunch, I saw Bryant and the other amigos at one table and at another table I saw three new jack officers filling out reports on the incident. They had nothing to do with it, but by writing the report they were admitting that they were there and that in some way were responsible for that inmate ending up in the hospital. I know this trick. Supervisors get the new jacks to take responsibility for the incident because they have less time on the job, which means there's more room for error. And supervisors need enforcers like me to stay off the reports.

Bryant gestured for me to come over and sit with them, so I did. The first thing that came out of her mouth was "How does it feel to be the talk of the jail right now?" I asked her what she meant.

"Come on now, you know everybody heard about the smack-down!" she says.

"Oh," I say, and shrug as if it was nothing.

"Yep, they're gonna use you, big man, you and aaaall yoouur muskels!" CO Z. Jones chimed in.

They laugh.

"Seriously, you better be careful, because you may be getting props right now but when shit hits the fan a lot of times you're gonna find yourself by yourself," Bryant says.

I ask her what she means and she says that now that they see that I'm not afraid to get my hands dirty they're going to be calling on me to handle inmate problems without it being an alarm.

"Watch and see," she says, "every time they want to handle an inmate and keep it on the low, these supervisors are going to be asking you to take a walk with them."

I just looked at her and said, "Hmm," as if I was listening to her. Truthfully, my mind was still on what just happened with Biz. She went on, not realizing that I was half-ass listening to her, and said, "I am telling you"—she raised her eyebrows—"these muthafuckas be running around here smacking these mates up until they run into one that's a scrapper and fights their asses back. Then they really put the beats on them and the mate winds up in the clinic with one of the staff that ain't a part of the team and ain't just gonna put down in their report that the inmate quote unquote"—she made the gesture with her fingers—"slipped in the shower. Then at the hospital all kinds of questions start to pop up, like how his jaw, ribs, and arm got broken from one fall? Then investigations are launched. And don't let the inmate be smart enough to remember one of y'all's badge numbers and name. You know some of y'all ain't smart enough to take your shield off or at least cover it up before y'all get into some shit. You're going to find yourself sitting down with the rest of the so-called goon squad trying to get the story together so that everybody is saying the same thing. A lot of times it's nothing and y'all get away with it because an inmate's family may not have money for a lawyer, but the few times that they do and can follow up with a lawsuit"—she pauses, then says—"it becomes every man for himself and you'll find yourself by yourself standing in front of a judge fighting for your job or worse, jail time."

At this point, she saw that she had my full attention. She saw the seriousness on my face. I mean the scared seriousness. My face went from "Big Hey putting in that work" to "Uh-uh, wasn't me. I wasn't there."

"Don't get shook nooooow, niggy!" she said.

They laugh again.

"I really don't think that you have anything to worry about, because how many of these dumb muthafuckas actually smart enough to put that lawyer and bail money away ahead of the jewelry, the cars, and the bitches?" she said.

I look at her like I don't know.

"Besides," she continues, "everyone knows that as a CO in here, we're like God."

I look at her with one eyebrow up, questioning what she just said, and she explains.

"Listen, if you get into some shit and you got a real muthafuckin' supervisor, I mean one that came up through the ranks, that didn't get put into position by way of a family member that has pull, that is an officer's supervisor, your ass is good. That kind of supervisor will know what to tell you to write in your report. That kind will know who to get to sign off on anything that we say happened in an incident, use of force or whatever. We have the power to manipulate the system and can get away with just about anything up in here."

While she's sitting there with a smirk on her face, I say, "God, huh?"

"Yep. We control these inmates' lives," she says. "They can't eat, shit, or wipe their ass without us giving them permission."

Then she looks at me with one eyebrow up and says, "Me, in particular, I like the fact that as a woman I get to tell a black man what to do and if he doesn't do it I can get his ass kicked at will."

They laugh and smack hands. Then Jones says, "Once they come through those doors we decide whether they're going to live in this bitch or whether they are going to fuck around with one of us and die up in this piece. Now, if that don't make me God up in here, then I am one of his cousins."

CHAPTER 19

VISITORS

"All days report! All days report!" I heard someone say as I walked to the front of the jail.

It was the end of my tour and all I wanted to do was to get out of this funky joint. As I got closer to the exit, I noticed that a hard-nosed female captain had taken a stance blocking the door with a podium. This meant that she could see any officer trying to leave without reporting to her first. She would check to see if she had any post open for mandatory overtime before the officer could leave. Corrections officers work on a four-day workweek with two days off. Today was my last day of working four days straight. Now it was my weekend. Since today was my last, I was a prime candidate to be stuck with overtime. *Fuck that!* I had to find a way out. *Think, Gee, think.* Got it. I could always sneak out through the visitors' area, because they have their own entrance that allows visitors to come and go.

So I make a beeline straight to the visitors' area, and once I get there I see the usual, a bunch of lying-ass inmates preparing to go see their loved ones. You have the Chameleons, the inmates who blend in with their surroundings—today they're Bloods, tomorrow they're Crips. Then they turn Muslim during Ramadan, in order to get some of the good food they have.

Then you have Balboas. These are the ones who come to the visits with black eyes and bruises from constantly getting their ass kicked by other inmates, yet tell their families that they took on four COs and won.

Then you have the Impostors. These inmates come on the visits faithfully to see their wife and kids every week. You see them hugging and kissing their loved ones and reassuring them that everything is okay, but on the flipside they are really being housed in the alternative-style housing unit, aka the "Homo House." After conversing with some of these inmates, I found a lot of them to be delusional, because for some strange reason they feel that if they're the ones doing the fucking and not the ones being fucked they're not gay. I walk by shaking my head and grimacing, because I know some of these men are living a gay lifestyle here in jail and after their sentence will go home to their unsuspecting wives or girlfriends as if everything was normal.

I walk up to the officers' station through a long corridor where chairs are lined up on each side with inmates who have changed out of their clothes into gray visitor-floor jumpsuits. I nod to the visit officer for him to press the button and unlock the sliding door that leads to the visitors' floor. He acknowledges me by raising his eyebrows and giving me a look like, "Don't let the captain see you." I nod back like, "I got you."

The door slides open and I walk onto the visitors' floor, where you hear nothing but loud conversations. Everybody is talking loud so that they can be heard. I walk by and say what's up to a couple of officers, who already know what I am up to. I slap them five and keep it moving as they hit a switch that opens another sliding door that leads down a flight of steps to where the visitors are preparing to come up to the visitors' floor. When I get down there it is chaos, as usual. You see the hustle and bustle for lockers by the visitors. You have the little kids running around unattended, and you hear the occasional complaint from a female visitor, "Why can't he have these pictures of me?" The male officer responds, while skimming through them again and again, "Ma'am, you're nude." She sucks her teeth in disgust, snatches the pictures, and calls him a hater. I chuckle, because he's a good officer. Normally, another officer would let the flicks in but they would never make it to the designated inmate.

As I'm making my way through the area I finally get the attention of the officer with the keys to let me out. Then I get a tap on my shoulder. I hear someone with a strong Jamaican accent saying, "Wheeerre ya tink ya goorin, Mr. Eerwood?" I knew it was the captain even before I turned around. I had to think fast.

"I was checking the doors to make sure that they were locked. We don't need no one slipping away, Cap," I said quickly with a smile.

She folded her arms and stood back with this don't-try-and-play-me look.

"Ya wooden be try-yain to pull a Hoooudini in me eerea, wood ya, Mr. Eerwood?" she said.

I give her the I-am-busted smile; then she says, "Me know dis ta be true 'cause em not assigned to me eerea." She smiles and continues, "Come wit' me now."

Then she grabs my hand and leads me toward her office.

"Me need you to do me a feerva if ya want seek pa-sage tru me eerea," she says.

"Anything, Cap," I say. *Just let me get the hell up out of here.*

When we get to her office, I see another female officer sitting at a desk filling out paperwork, and to her left, sitting in the corner, is a young black female holding a baby and rocking it back and forth.

The girl is crying hysterically. She screams out at me, "Please, Mister. I won't do it again!" The baby reacts to her screaming and starts to cry. The captain says, "Me need you to woch er for one sec-con while de officer writes er report till me get back." She steps out of the office and the girl continues to scream and cry, holding her baby tight, asking me, "What are they going to do to me? What are they going to do to my baby?" I pause, then answer, "I don't know." She stands up and grabs my arm, with the baby dangling in her other arm, and pleads, "Please don't let them take her from me. I swear I won't do it again. I swear."

I motion for her to sit back down, then I gesture for her to calm down. She sits and starts rocking again with her baby held tight. I go over to the desk and the officer starts to fill me in on what happened. She states that while she was patrolling the visitors' floor she noticed that this young lady and the inmate kept passing the baby back and forth to each other, which most times would be normal, but then she noticed that every time the inmate had the baby he would stick his finger between the baby's thighs into the diaper. I notice that the female officer is telling me all this while looking at the young girl in total disgust. She goes on, saying that those moves from the inmate raised a red flag and she escorted the couple off the visitors' floor. The inmate was searched, and drugs were found between his butt cheeks. He was attempting to commit an act called boofing. Boofing is when an inmate secretes a hidden item inside his rectum.

The officer searched the girl and nothing was found, but the baby was crying loudly and appeared irritated. The officer decided to search the baby and found two more bundles of drugs stashed inside the diaper. While the officer is telling me the story, the girl holds her head down in shame. I know what is going to happen next but can't bring myself to admit it to the girl. She is going to be arrested and the Child Protection Agency will take the child.

When the captain returned with the authorities, the theatrics began again. The girl jumped up and started crying, continuing to hold on to her baby, but to no avail, because there would be no mercy here. The police took the baby from her and handed it to a woman dressed in businesslike attire, and the girl began yelling and screaming and struggling to reach for her baby. The police wrestled her down to the ground and put handcuffs on her and then the baby started to cry and to reach for her. As she was led out on display, the loud visitors' room became a library, as everyone stopped talking and parted like the Red Sea to allow the shame parade to walk past.

CHAPTER 20

RIDE-OR-DIE CHICK

When they left, I hurry up and scoot my ass out through the door with them. I go to the front entrance of my jail, get my weapon from the arsenal, and am like a blue blur getting to my van. Once inside, I start it up and do my ritual, reaching inside my glove compartment and grabbing a small bottle of liquor so that I can wind down and reflect on the happenings of the day. As I sip, I think, *What was that chick thinking?* I mean, what did she think was going to happen if she got caught? I shake my head as I pull out of the parking lot and get in line with the other officers' cars trying to leave the Island.

Was it worth it?

Was that love?

Is that what being a ride-or-die chick is all about?

Now what?

You in jail.

He in jail.

And the baby is now being handled by strangers for the time being.

Your man, that you were bringing the drugs to, is now going to be hit with more charges, so it's safe to say he will be doing more time.

84

Maybe she did it because when he was home he held her down and whatever he was doing for them landed him in jail. That's the only reason that I can think of that would prompt someone to risk her life like that. I put the top on the bottle that I am sipping from and put it between my legs as I pull up to the security officer assigned to search every vehicle that leaves the Island. Since I have a minivan he looks inside and signals for me to keep it moving. I pull off, grab my bottle, and unscrew the cap with one hand and start sipping while I drive across the only bridge on the Island leading to the other side. I think to myself, *Some people don't have their priorities right.* That girl should have told her man that if he really loved her he would not have her risk herself and their baby just to bring that shit inside the jail for him. She was cute, too. Normally, these inmates find an ugly or fat female or a female with low self-esteem to bring it in for them. They lie to them with promises of being with them when they come out, conning them to do anything from bringing in stuff to the occasional blowjob on the visitors' floor. I sip some more while driving with one hand and imagine one inmate sitting there with his moms visiting him and another inmate right next to him getting head.

I hit the highway and make it around to my block in no time. I stop by the local liquor store to get another half pint, then proceed to walk to my projects. I tuck my bottle inside my pocket before I pass my homeys standing on the corner, because, you know, the liquor store always gives you those distinctive black bags with the gold flowers on them, a dead giveaway in the streets. *Negroes won't have proper ID but they will always have a cup for a drink.* I say, "Whatup," and breeze to my building. When I get to my building I go to the mailbox to get the mail. Then from behind me I hear, "Boy, you gaining weight?" I turn around. I'm stuck. It's Ms. Daniels, Biz's mother. She comes over to me in her usual way with her arms extended for me to give her a hug, the same way we've done since I was a kid. I hug her and try to keep a straight face. We get on the elevator together and she starts to talk, asking me where my moms is and about them singing in the choir this coming Sunday. She is not facing me when she's talking, so she can't see me with my elevator-please-hurry-up face.

Then she goes where I knew she would. She starts talking about Brian, Biz's real name. She tells me that he had gotten in some trouble in his assigned jail and that they transferred him to another one. Shaking her head, she says, "That boy just can't seem to stay out of trouble." Then she turns to me and says, "I know your momma sho is proud a you, the way you turned out, and I am proud of you, too."

"Thank you, Ms. Daniels."

The elevator opens up on her floor and before she gets out she says, "I hope that my baby ends up over there where you work at because I know that you will keep an eye on him for me and make sure that he is safe so that I don't have to worry so much about him." Then she turns and looks at me, and I can see that she is tired and worn down with him going in and out of jail the way he does. She steps off the elevator and before it closes she says, "If ya happen to run into him, could ya tell him that I love him and that I am here for him but I am getting too old and I don't know how much longer I can take this."

"Okay, Ms. Daniels."

Then she walks away and yells, "You be good now, ya hear!" The elevator closes and goes to my floor. That I am feeling like shit is an understatement. *How could I have let this happen?* And trust me when I tell you that half that bottle of liquor is gone before I stick the key in the door. I get inside and drop the mail on the table for my mother, and without even looking up at me she starts in.

"You ain't take out the garbage when you left this morning and you left those dirty dishes in the sink again. Boy, I am tired of cleaning up behind you!"

I just put my head down and go to my room. Once inside I get comfortable and finish off the rest of my bottle. I can hear Moms on the warpath about my lack of attention to the cleanliness of her house. I sit there and think that that's the problem with the families of officers: They don't ever think about the type of job that we do or think about the type of day that we might have had in our line of work. I am well sauced up now and all my emotions are about to boil over. I stand up, about to yell back at her through the door. I am about to say, "Listen here, woman," but then I think better of it and rationalize that even with the gun I have, I stand no chance against the Birmingham battle cat from Alabama. It would be straight suicide.

I fall back onto my bed and ask myself if it can get any worse than this. Then at that moment, she opens my door without knocking. I look at her like, *I could have been naked!* She flings a piece of mail at me and slams the door, and as she walks away she yells, "That was slid under the front door when I came in, and besides, you ain't got nothing I ain't seen before, boy!" I sit there for a moment staring at the door as if she is standing there and can see me. I open the letter to see it's from my baby momma and at that moment things just get worse. It is a court order to pay child support. *Damn.* I sit there drunk and lie back on my bed with the letter on my stomach with my eyes half closed. My windows are wide open and I do not hear a peep. I mean no gunshots, no police or fire truck sirens, nothing. Even my moms stops beefing. I get up, put my gun on my minitable, and start taking it apart to clean it, because as far as I can remember, it's always quiet before the storm.

CHAPTER 21

CHILD SUPPORT

"Let me see, umm, this is from last Christmas, and this one is from her school clothes last year."

A few months have gone by and now I'm sitting in the waiting area at Child Support Court. I have receipts in my mouth, and in both hands, and the Timberland shoe box sitting on my lap. I brought all these special-occasion-holiday-dad receipts in order to prove to the judge that I take care of my kids. I take a look around and all I see is a lot of hate and anger on the faces of men and smiles and chitchat among the women. I see my wife sitting by herself a few benches down from me. We had been going back and forth to court for months, delaying the process, because of concerns due to her pregnancy. After she had the baby, which was not mine, she could make the court date. I wasn't mad that she had a baby by another man, because I knew that I was running through the jails swinging my dick from left to right. She and I were on speaking terms for the kids' sake and that was it. My situation was not like most COs' situations, where due to mandatory overtime they're never home and the spouses tend to stray.

I was sitting there nervous with my heart pounding and sweat rolling down from my unkempt hair with a little Jheri curl juice rolling down with it. I thought about all the horror stories that I'd heard from other COs. One CO that I knew had quit the job and gotten a McDonald's job, because it was no longer worth it for him to come to work due to the garnishment. Another went and tried to kill his spouse, and now he's doing time. I remember when I first got on the job and I was sitting in the officers' cafeteria when a female officer came over to the table where I was sitting and started coming on to me. She was telling me how big and handsome I was and that she would spend a lot of money on me if I became her boy toy. I was flattered until I noticed that she was talking loud enough for everyone in the area to hear it. Then she stood up and started yelling and pointing at another male officer that was sitting at another table across from us, saying, "That's right! I tricks that money I get from this nigga here every month, aaalll fourteen hundred of it! Yeeeeah, and it ain't shit he can do about it." She then walked by him, leaving other officers laughing and leaving me sitting there looking stupid. I sat there grimacing at the thought of ending up like him.

I wonder to myself why my wife decided to take me to Child Support Court. I mean, I bought the kids school clothes. Every Christmas or birthday either I or one of the grandmothers bought them gifts. So they were always taken care of one way or another. I give myself a look-over. Messed-up haircut, check. Bummy clothes on, check. No jewelry and unshaved, check and check. And most important, my Timberland shoe box full of please-be-enough-to-save-my-ass receipts, check. I had been advised by other officers not to come to court appearing to have a lot of money or seem well-off.

At this time the court officer comes out and calls out our names. We both stand up and walk over to the entrance. I give a hand gesture like *ladies first* and she proceeds. Once we get inside the courtroom we are ushered to stand behind a table that is equipped with two microphones. The judge instructs us to state our names. We do, and the festivities begin.

The judge states that we are here to settle the issue of child support for our kids and then he states their names. I get an uneasy feeling about the way he says "we" but has his eyes, which are peeking over glasses, focused just on "me." Then he states that we have been coming back and forth with this issue and that we hope to resolve it today. My wife had missed a couple of dates due to her pregnancy, so the judge asks me if I accept her excuse for missing the dates and I say, "Yes." I figure that if I say no she will go and petition for child support all over again anyway, so let's just get this shit over with.

The judge asks me to present the items that the court ordered me to bring. I take the papers out of my shoe box. I fix them neatly, then hand them to the court officer.

"Mr. Heyward, are your W-2 and pay stubs in this pile of papers?" asks the judge sarcastically.

"Yes, sir," I say.

"Good," he says. "So that way we won't waste time."

He pulls out those two pieces of paper and brushes the rest to the side. Then he starts in on his large calculator and all you hear is him punching those buttons a mile a minute. I get a little agitated because it seems like he is not going to consider the receipts that provide proof of my efforts to be a father to my kids.

"Excuse me, Your Honor, those are my receipts for all of the money I spent on my kids," I say.

At that moment, as soon as those stupid ass words come out of my mouth, I know that I have fucked up.

"Mr. Heyward, it appears to me that you have been misinformed," he says, peering out at me. "We are not here to see if you're going to pay child support, because that's already been decided.

We are here to decide how much you will contribute toward the well-being of your kids."

Then he takes his off glasses and continues, "So many times I have witnessed father after father come into my courtroom with folders, briefcases, and of course shoe boxes filled with receipts, trying to prove that they are fit fathers to their children. I see the receipts but then I don't see them, because a real father would never have to prove something that he should be doing naturally. You think a bunch of receipts is going to prove to me that you spend time with your kids? That you go to parent-teacher meetings or attend a school play now and then?" I tried to interject, saying, "But I be at work all the time." He gave me a look like, "Muthafucka, I did not ask you to speak." He laid into me again.

"Mr. Heyward," he asks, "how much cash do you give to her on a monthly basis?"

"Well," I stutter, "I buy the kids clothes and stuff and uumm—"

"Oh, I see," he cuts me off, "you're one of them. You're one of those if-they-need fathers, instead of an all-the-time father."

He sees that I have a confused look on my face and he breaks it down for me.

"If the child needs shoes, you buy them shoes. If the child needs clothes, you buy them clothes. But when the next month comes, you figure that you don't have to provide any finances because they should not need anything. Well, you're wrong! She needs money for food and rent and unexpected expenses that may come up."

I am livid by this time and blurt out, "What about her? I mean, aren't we supposed to be doing this together?"

"She is doing her part," he says. "She has to tend to their every need while you're out there"—he pauses and looks me up and down as if he knows that I am full of shit—"working."

Then he goes back to punching his calculator and figuring out how much of my ass he is going to BITE OFF. When he comes back with the numbers, I shit on myself. Then it gets worse, because I had already accepted her reason for missing those court dates. That bites me in my ass some more. He hits the calculator again, punching those fucking buttons. *I hate that fucking calculator.* He then says that since I was so generous and pardoned her for missing those dates, I am actually awarding her arrears from the first day that she petitioned. This move adds more money to my biweekly payment and basically shreds my income.

"What about me?" I lose it. "How am I supposed to survive?" I yell.

The court officer, who has foreseen this and has already requested assistance, comes and grabs me by the arm. His partner takes my other arm and they begin to escort me out of the courtroom. As we walk by the judge's desk, they pick up my papers and proceed to the door. Then they put my papers on my chest for me to hold. I look back over my shoulder to say something else to the judge, but he is already busy preparing for his next victim and doesn't even look up.

As I am waiting for the elevator, pacing back and forth, the door to the waiting room opens and out comes one of the court officers who escorted me out. He yawns and walks over to the garbage can and throws something in it. It is my shoe box. It lands in a pile of about thirty others.

CHAPTER 22

THIRTY-NINE DOLLARS

A few weeks have passed since I was in court.

"Hold up, hold up, there must be some mistake!" I say as I bang on the window of our personnel office, where we retrieve our paychecks.

I look at my check. Thirty-nine dollars. I'm banging on the window like I hit the number in the streets and the number man is somewhere in there hiding so he won't have to pay me!

"Yo, Lopez, open up!" I yell out.

An officer opens the window and starts to complain, "We're closed. It's payday. You know that we're closed." I'm standing there sweating, looking at him with a wrinkled forehead and bulging eyes like I don't give a fuck what day it is, *Y'all best ta get me my money!* He sees the serious expression on my face and says, "What is it?" like he's tired and has things to do. I say, "Y'all fucked up my check again!" He asks for my check stub and I give it to him. He goes over it and hands it back to me, asking if I took a look at it. I say, "No. The only thing that I saw was that thirty-nine muthafucking dollars and I knew that y'all had fucked up some kind of way."

"Rif!" he says.

"What?" I say.

"Reading Is Fundamental!" he answers.

"The fuck you talking about?" I ask.

"If you read the bottom, it shows you that she has gotten an increase," he says.

"An increase?" I ask.

He says, "Yes, ever' so often the mother of your kids can go to court and get an increase due to the cost of living always changing. So that's what that is. The thirty-nine dollars ain't permanent, it's just until the system catches the payments up and levels it out." As professional and as cordial as he is, I still didn't like what he was saying. I turn to walk away and hear him yell as he slams the window down, "Don't spend it in one place!" I storm out of the area, cursing to myself, "This is some bullshit. How do they expect me to live? I have rent to pay, my car note, and other bills! How am I supposed to make it?"

As I'm walking down the corridor on my way to my post, I see an inmate that I know from the streets. These run-ins are now happening on a regular basis. He says, "What's up?" then winks and says, "Whenever you're ready, Wood." I am not in the mood for his begging me to bring something in for him, so I blow him off by picking up my pace and saying, "Yeah, yeah." If I had a dollar for every time an inmate approached me and tried to get me to bring in something for him I would be rich. These inmates feel comfortable asking an officer to bring them shit because writing them up for asking has no effect on anything. It's just more work for the officer. I immediately return my focus to more pressing issues, like my money!

I arrive on my post and I see that my partner for the day is Officer Parks, a good friend of mine, but more important, a drinking buddy—and that's just what I need. As soon as I get on post I regulate these muthafuckas. I yell out for them not to ask me for shit and tell them that they're dead today on getting anything because I ain't in the mood for no bullshit. I hear grumbling for a few minutes, then they go back to watching television and working out. After the supervisor makes his tour, Officer Parks does his usual and breaks out his water bottle, and let's just say Poland Springs ain't never made water that tastes like this. We start sipping and I start venting about my child support situation.

"Yo, Parks, I don't know how I am going to make it," I say to him. "Ever since I got hit with this shit I've been running myself ragged trying to make ends meet. Check it, I do overtime whenever they have it and I moonlight on my days off doing unauthorized security at the local clothing stores. This shit has me doing risky bullshit just to stay afloat. Sheeit, the other day I almost got jumped by a couple of dudes trying to steal clothes from the store. I'm fighting and tussling with these muthafuckas over a shirt and I am only getting a buck a day!"

"So what did you do?" he asks me.

"I let the muthafuckas go and they hauled ass up out of there," I say.

We both laugh. I fill my cup up again and continue.

"I was doing all kinds of kamikaze shit like working two shifts here from seven a.m. until eleven p.m."—of course, sleeping most of my second tour, letting whatever inmate had the most power run the housing area—"on my last day before I get my two days off, then leaving from here, going straight to a strip joint up in the Bronx, working there till the morn...nin...ng..." I say.

My words begin to slur, because a brother is feeling no pain. My face is numb and little beads of sweat are coming down the sides of it.

"I had to give the strip joint up because one time while I was checking IDs of everyone coming in, a stripper who worked there showed me her high school ID card. So I denied her entry. The owner went crazy, saying that she was his best moneymaker. That was the last time I did that. I was not going to be responsible if that place got raided."

At this time an inmate comes up to the bubble (the officers' station) and asks for toilet tissue. I bark on him and say, "You ain't getting shit! Go wipe yo ass with your hand!" Then I continue my conversation while he stands there for a moment staring at me. He storms off saying something that I can't hear but that draws the attention of the other inmates. I don't like that shit. He storms back up to the bubble with the inmate rule book in his hand, waving it in the air, yelling and going off about what he's entitled to and so on, drawing more attention to the situation. He starts ranting and raving about how we as officers use our power to take advantage of them and treat them like slaves but don't realize that we are the real Uncle Toms doing the white man's dirty work for him by oppressing our own people. Now he has my blood boiling, ruining my peaceful tour with this bullshit, so I get back at him, saying, "Is it my fault!? Huh! Is it my fault you robbed that old lady!? Huh, or sold them drugs!?" Then I hit him with the ultimate insult. "Oh, or maybe you're one of the ones that like to play with little boys."

The response to this remark from the other inmates enrages him. He comes back, saying, "Y'all come up in here like y'all better than us!" I counter, "I am!" He continues, "Like just because we committed a crime you as a CO can shit on us and violate our rights!" I'm hyped and drunk. I come back at him, "I am the fuckin' judge. Is it my fault that you got caught? I didn't put you here. You put you here! Don't blame me because you put yourself in the position for me to treat you like a slave." He comes back with "You're supposed to be a corrections officer but what are you correcting?" Then he mimics me, "Wipe yo ass with yo hand!" He starts waving the inmate rule book toward me, yelling, "What are you correcting? Did they teach you that in the Academy? Tell me that ain't some master-to-slave shit!" Now he has an audience and continues, "Did they train you in the Academy on how to correct somebody and make them a better citizen when they come home?" He answers himself, "No, so why do they call y'all correctional officers?"

I see the other inmates nodding in agreement. He sees it and now he feels that he's on a roll. He's now standing there with his arms folded when he says to me sarcastically, "The judge didn't say for you to further punish us after we were sentenced. And it ain't even the crackers here on the Island, it's our own kind that do it to us." He throws the rule book in my direction; it hits the gate that separates us as he walks off back to his cell. Now I am really pissed! I'm pissed that this muthafucka got the best of me, that the child support judge got the best of me, and that I have a thirty-nine-dollar check in my pocket and there ain't shit I can do about it. I open the gate and storm in behind him. My partner does the ultimate no-no and comes in behind me, ordering all the inmates to go inside the day room. This move is crazy, because even though we have our body alarms that alert the officers in the control room, if we are in trouble and need assistance, we have the keys to let them in. We are both now on the floor with the inmates, who could kill us both before anybody can get there to help us. I go down the walkway to the inmate's cell and when I get there he's standing inside it with a smirk on his face like, *Whatcha want to do?* I don't hesitate and neither does he; we lunge at each other. We both swing, him hitting me in the chest, and me hitting him on the side of his head.

Now all I see is that judge's face and all I hear is the tapping on the keys of that fucking calculator adding up my money. I black out on him and start punching wildly, screaming, "I take care of my fucking kids!" He looks at me, confused, but does not stop putting up a fight. Good, because I don't want him to. I want this right now. No, I need this right now. I want to hit something, somebody, anybody, and he is the prime candidate. He catches me on the side of my jaw. Pow! I don't feel shit. My face is numb. I head butt him and he goes down. I grab the judge in a choke hold from behind. He grabs at my arms, trying to break free. He can't. I start yelling over and over again, "I take care of my fucking kids!" In my head all I hear now are voices echoing, *A REAL FATHER DOES NOT HAVE TO PROVE HE'S A REAL FATHER!*

The next thing I know, my partner is yelling at me to let him go because his face is losing color. I do, and the inmate drops to the floor holding his neck and gasping for air. I step over him, leaving him there on the floor, and my partner backs up my attitude by throwing the inmate rule book back at the inmate and slamming his cell door closed. We walk back to the officers' station. My partner yells for an inmate named Murder, the local gang leader who runs all the inmates, to go and check on our civil rights leader. We sit down and he, like the caring coworker that he is, pours me another drink, along with one for himself. Then he lays into me. "Muthafucka, are you crazy? You could have killed that nigga. Now I am all for backing up my partner no matter what but I ain't about to throw my shit away on some bullshit like this!" He continues, "You better get a hold of yourself with this child support shit, because it will back you into a corner and have you doing wild shit that you would not normally do." Murder came back and told us that Mandela was okay and just wanted to know if he could get some hot water for his soup. Parks lets him out and he comes past the officers' station and yells, "It's all good, CO, 'cause I jails for real. Ain't no snitching here." I nod and he goes and gets his hot water. Parks tells me that most likely Murder warned him not to make the house hot by going to the clinic. I chill out the rest of my tour, then bounce. I change my clothes and wait for the route bus to take me from the jail to the officers' parking lot. While waiting for the bus I overhear another officer bragging about his new phone that has a calculator in it. I look over at him like, *If he only knew what I want to do to that phone right now.*

CHAPTER 23

HOOD BOOGAS

"No, poppie, please noooo! Please don't take it. I need it!"

"Ma'am, you're going to have to let it go!"

"Poppie, please, my back. I have back pains. I can't sleep without this bed."

Me and my partner were at this Spanish (anyone who speaks Spanish—Mexicans, Dominican, Puerto Rican, etc.) lady's apartment. She was pleading with us not to take the box spring and mattress while I was holding up the bed and my partner was prying her fingers off. I shook my head, wondering to myself, *What kind of stupid shit have I gotten myself into?* My partner was hearing none of it. He continued to yank the bed out of her apartment and down the hall to the elevator. She crumpled to the floor and continued to sob out loud and to curse us out in Spanish. I stepped over her and went down the hall to help my partner put the items into the elevator.

"Yo, do you think that we should have at least let her keep the mattress?" I asked my partner.

"Shiiiiiiit, that's a hundred muthafuckin' dollars!" he said. "Do you have a hundred dollars in yo pocket right now?"

I shook my head no.

"A'ight then!" he said.

Then we continued to push and cram the items into the elevator. I took one last look down the hall at the woman. She was sitting on the floor in front of her apartment crying. I shook my head in disgust at myself because I knew that I knew better. And, oh yeah, did I mention that she was seven months pregnant?

Here I was now on another suicide mission, another part-time job, trying to make a buck. I teamed up with a store that rents out items to people with bad credit. My job was to retrieve the items when the renter couldn't make the monthly payment.

The routine went like this: I knocked on the apartment door like I was the police. When the person inside looked through the peephole to see who was knocking, I showed my Corrections badge, which looks like a police officer's badge. The person inside opened the door, puzzled as to why the police were knocking on the door. At that moment a representative from the store stepped into view with the contract agreement in hand.

In most cases the client would slam the door in the representative's face. But because they thought a cop was standing right there they would give in and let us retrieve the items. I'd stand there with my badge around my neck (of course with my name and numbers taped up so that they could not be seen) and my firearm exposed at my side. Every now and then we would have to put some extra icing on the cake by using radios and police jargon, like "Yes, we have the suspect in sight," and "Have the backup stand by in case of resistance." Once they heard the response on the other end, "Ten-four," they threw their hands up and gave in.

After the Spanish lady we continued to retrieve items from the remaining apartments on our list. By the end of the day, we had made out pretty good. Well, that is, up until we made our last stop. My partner and I were outside an apartment where we had just successfully run our routine.

The routine started off pretty good. My partner and I were standing outside adding up what we were getting paid. "Let's see, we get one hundred dollars if we get the items and fifty dollars just for knocking on the doors of the not-at-homes," he said. We also received hazardous-duty pay. That's for when we show our badges in these neighborhoods where the people behind the door may have warrants or be drug dealers and think that we came there to apprehend them.

We were standing there and all of a sudden the worker from the store came running out of the building. He jetted by us and jumped into the car, leaving me and my partner standing in front of the building dumbfounded.

We walked over to the car, got in, and asked him what happened. But before he could say anything, two actual police cars, with sirens wailing, pulled up to the building. The police jumped out with guns drawn and ran into the building. I waited until they were all the way in the building, then I peeled off down the block, getting out of there. After we collected our money, my partner slapped the shit out of the worker for not telling us that the tenant called the cops on two people impersonating the police. That was the end of that gig, because later on we found out that other cops had gotten fired for doing the same thing for this store.

It was late when we got off that day. I made a mad dash to get my medication—yep, from the liquor store. I bought a half gallon of Hennessy and was on my way to see a "hood booga." (A hood booga is any low-self-esteem female in any hood who is on welfare with a bunch of kids, who has no job, no goals, no ambitions, and who is comfortable with lounging around all day collecting her food stamps, who will give up the cookie to any city employee because he has benefits . . . yeah, I said it!) These were the females that I preyed on, because when you're going through something and have long hard days at work you need a three-hole-minimum-requirement, down-for-whatever-sex-you-desire type of female. Personally, I think women like this need a holiday named after them.

On my way to her house, I stop to get the equipment I need.

Bag of weed. Check.

Chicken wings and French fries. Check.

Condoms. Check! Check!

Oh yeah, I almost forgot, a big ole bag of sunflower seeds that she can eat all day while watching television.

It's close to three in the morning when I get to her house. I hear the music blasting when I get off the elevator. Hey, why not, she doesn't have to get up in the morning. I knock on the door and I hear her yelling at her kids as she unlocks it, "Y'all better go to bed! Taquan, I told you to move your toys out the hallway!" I thought, *Great, the kids are up and don't they have school in the morning?* She opens the door with nothing on but a T-shirt and a joint in her hand. I don't do drugs and I hate smoking cigarettes, weed—it's all the same to me.

"Hey, boo," she says.

"What's up, baby," I say.

She goes to give me a kiss and I turn my head. She gets the side of my face. She's not offended. She knows what it is. I go inside and it's the normal setting. There's a couch and a television, with toys and bags of unwashed clothes on the living room floor. I give her the bag of weed and the chicken. She says, "Thank you. They ain't had nothing to eat all day." Then she goes into the room with her kids. I hear her instructing them to stay in there and go to bed after they finish eating the chicken wings. I take off my jacket, sit on the couch, and get comfortable. I open the liquor and start drinking it from the bottle. She comes back with her cup and fills it up. It doesn't take long before I am feeling nice and can tolerate the strong weed smoke.

She's still smoking when she gets down on her knees between my legs and starts to unzip my pants. She pulls me out and starts to kiss on me between puffs and I don't even care because I pick the bottle up and take it to the head for a couple of seconds, letting the air bubbles flow back into the bottle. Now she has me in her mouth and, one-handed, unbuckles my belt. I take my gun out of the holster and place it by me on the couch. With my pants now down by my ankles, she goes to work and the shit feels so good. I grab the back of her head and start to drift in and out thinking about my life right now. I'm so tired of all these crazy jobs that I'm doing now to stay afloat. I hadn't really seen my kids. I'm not sure if it's from working so much or my resentment from my kids' mother taking me to court.

Damn, this shit feels good. I open my eyes to watch her performance. Then all of a sudden her youngest child comes running into the living room. She stops in mid-goggle and I half-ass sit up, but she nudges me to lean back with one hand still around me. She yells for him to get back in that room and go to bed. He looks at her, grabs his favorite stuffed animal off the floor, and runs back into the room. She continues her assault and before long I am releasing my tadpoles into her mouth to seek out her tonsils. Then she stands me up and I grab the bottle and my gun and hold up my pants as she pulls me past the kids' room and into her bedroom.

There we knock all the clothes off the bed and onto the floor and get butt naked. I drink some more from the jug as I admire her body. She takes off her shirt and climbs up on the bed on all fours. She has big flabby tits and a gut to go along with a big round cheddar cheese cellulite butt. To put it short, I am in heaven. I mount her and quickly get into a rhythm and all you hear is the cranking from her raggedy bed. I slip out and proceed to put it in her third hole and as I look down to get into position I see that my condom popped. I don't care because I am so gone now and this tight shit feels so good that I just can't stop! She moans and says, "Damn, baby, that feels good. You fit right in there." *Is that a compliment or an insult?* Now I'm vigorously hitting it. I am up on my tippy toes so that I can hit it at a better angle. I'm sweating and farting and shit and I have her bent over with her gut on the bed. My gut is on her back. Her titties flapping. My titties flapping. This is bliss. I reach down and pick up the bottle and drink. I got Hennessy pouring out from the side of my mouth and dripping down my chest.

As I am still hitting it, I bring the bottle down and for the first time I notice the large mirror that she has on her dresser. The view of myself that I see is disgusting. I think to myself, *You're not living right. Your job situation is out of control and you're a drunk.* I can hear my momma say, "You ought to be ashamed of yourself." Right then she tightens up on me. I grunt "uhhh" and any remorse or guilt that I was feeling just skates right out of me.

CHAPTER 24

ROCK BOTTOM

Boom! Boom! Boom!

I'm awakened by my mother banging on my bedroom door. I look over at my clock and it says 2:30 a.m. I answer her, half asleep, "What's the matter?"

"There's somebody on the phone for you named Marshal," she says.

I'm puzzled and wondering why an officer from my job is calling me at this time of morning. I make my way to the phone and on the other end I hear, "Gary Heyward?" I say, "Yes," and the voice on the other end lets me know that he is the city marshal and he's in the parking lot about to repo my van. I put the phone down on the table. My heart sinks. I close my eyes and take a deep breath. My mother notices the look of despair on my face and asks me what happened. I momentarily ignore her question and pick the phone back up.

"Hello! Are you there?"

"I'm here."

"Well, I see that you have an officer's plaque in the window. So that's why I am giving you a courtesy call so that you can come down and get any personal items that you may have inside the vehicle."

"Thank you. I'm on my way down."

A few weeks have passed and all the suicide jobs have fallen through. All my resources to get money have dried up and the bills just keep piling up. I knew this day was coming. I was behind in my payments and I knew that I could not keep playing hide-and-seek with my van, parking it in different spots, praying that when I came out in the morning to go to work it would be there. Plus I owed about a gazillion dollars in parking tickets.

After I retrieved my items I stayed up until it was time for me to go to work. I had to use mass transit now and leave home at least an hour and a half earlier to get to work on time. I got dressed and left. I walked slowly to the bus stop because I didn't have a dime to my name, not even carfare to get to work. When the bus pulled up I took a deep breath because I knew that I was not supposed to be using my badge to get on for free, but I had no choice, and some bus drivers really act like they're paying your fare out of their pockets if they let a corrections officer on for free. But if I were an NYPD officer, no problem. Some of the drivers ask you to pull out your ID because our badges are so similar. I waited to be the last one so that the embarrassment would not be so bad if the driver gave me a hard time. He didn't and I breathed a sigh of relief and sat down. All the way to work I just kept thinking that something has got to give.

I arrived at work and took my post. It was my steady post, which meant no more rotating schedules and different times to be at work. I was assigned area 8 upper and my permanent hours were 7:00 a.m. to 3:00 p.m. It was bittersweet, though, because all the inmates in my area were high-classification inmates. So I had all murderers and drug kingpin types. I started my shift with Flocko in my face asking me if I was all right, because I didn't look so good. He started making jokes about me looking like a bum with my face unshaven, my hair not cut, and my bummy wrinkled uniform. I really had not noticed my appearance and didn't care, so I laughed at him, because we were real cool and I've known his whole family since we were kids. He had been trying to get me to bring him stuff in for a few months now, whenever he got the chance. Now that I was his area officer I knew that he would not stop, but I also knew that he knew how far to take it. He continued with his workout and I went back to doing my job and stressing about my situation. The day went on with me in and out of disbelief about no longer having a vehicle. I walked to the back of my housing area so that I could get a signal on my cell phone so I could check my messages. I was happy that I at least still had a phone.

BEEP, first message from my moms: "When you come home can you stop by the supermarket and pick up some butta beans? I thought I had some in the cabinet, and don't forget I need my change"—the rent—"this week."

BEEP, my moms again: "You got a letter from that loan you applied for; they said no because you had too many garnishments; also go to C-Town grocery store because they have the beans on sale and I don't like that manager of the other store on the corner."

BEEP, my baby momma: "Your daughter needs some sneakers, so could you get them this week? I didn't get my check yet" (my child support payment). After this message my blood began to boil. I thought about her words and repeated them: "My check!"

I knew that I had to take care of my kids, but the thought of her getting my money like that and her not having any accountability as to where my money was being spent just burned me up. I mean, she could be spending it on anything and anybody and it ain't shit I could do about it. The court was making sure that they kept track of me paying her, but no one was keeping track of how the money was being spent on my kids. How could she fix her mouth to say, "My check didn't come yet," as if she were in here with me dealing with murderers and shit?

My day dragged on and I went to check my messages again.

BEEP.

It's the hood booga telling me that she has some news for me . . . she's pregnant! I yell out, "Fuck!" Then I throw my phone against the wall and it shatters. This gets the attention of some inmates working out nearby. I put my hands on my head and pace back and forth. *Of all the stupid things for my dick to do at a time like this. This can't be happening. Let me think, let me think, did I cum in her?* I did remember wearing a rubber. I know I didn't go up in there raw smiggady. Damn, I needed to get to a phone.

I pick up the pieces to my phone and go to the officers' station to get an outside line. Frantically, I call the main control room so that they can give me an outside line and they connect me to the HB. I know that you're not supposed to talk your business on these lines but I am desperate and have to get to the bottom of this. Hood booga answers the phone and I say, "What's up?" Then she says, "Oh, you can't call nobody back? You been ignoring a bitch's call, but as soon as I tell you I am pregnant, bliiing, here you go!" I say, "Are you sure?" She says, "Yes, I am sure and before you come at me, nigga, it's yours."

I'm stuck. She continues, "I ain't got no coverage, so unless you give me the money for an abortion, I'm having it." I don't say anything at first. Then I tell her I'll call her after I get off work.

"Fuck, fuck, fuck!" Of all the stupid things that I've done in my life I go and make my shit worse.

I know this chick is lying. I can feel it, but what am I going to do? She's got me fucked up right now. I know I ain't about to have a baby with her and start this shit all over again, especially after what I am going through right now. I know she is definitely plotting on doing the child support thing with me. I begin to panic. *I got to get this money up.* I start to pace the floor again in the officers' station and then Flocko comes up to the station to ask if I can open the shower for him. I look at him for a long moment and he looks at me, puzzled, like, "Why are you looking at me like that?" I then tell him to go ahead in the shower. I sit back and take a look around me as if I am being watched. I know what I have to do. . . .

CHAPTER 25

DICK DILEMMA

"Seven hundred dollars, eight hundred, nine hundred, a G," says Hector, Flocko's brother.

I'm sitting in McDonald's on 145th Street and Broadway in Harlem. Time was running out; I desperately needed to get this abortion done. Tracy (a hood booga gets a name after she has a Negro by the balls) called me to say that she was feeling real sick and that the doctor told her that if she went through with this pregnancy it would be a difficult one. She was practically begging me for the abortion now. I was happy about that but stressing it, too, because I had to make money in order to get it done. Hector says, "Good looking out, G. We need more brothers like you on the inside because sometimes a person be in there under all that pressure and just needs help. Ya know what I mean?" *I most certainly do.*

"No prob. You know how far back we go," I tell him.

"Cool, tell my brother I love him," he says. He finishes eating his burger, then shakes my hand and bounces.

I sit there for a minute and look around the McDonald's to see if I recognize anybody. My conscience is telling me, "Negro, you ain't did nothing wrong yet. You only have money on you and nothing else." I realize this but I still have the jitters. My conscience: "Because you know this shit is wrong!" I shake off the feeling and call Tracy to tell her that I'm coming to get her, so she needs to get ready. I borrow a friend's car and take her to the clinic. When we park, she asks me for the money as if I'm not going inside with her. I let her know that I am not letting her go in there alone.

"We did this together, so we are going to handle it together," I say.

She looks at me as if to say the other guys never wanted to come inside. Then she smiles at me and says, "Thank you." *Woman, if you think that I am just going to hand you this money after all the shit I am going through to handle this situation, you must be crazy.* Besides, I needed to see this all the way through. Shit, if I could've been in there when the procedure was done, I would've been.

After it is all over, I feel relieved. I feel that I have dodged a major bullet. It was worth it. I was not about to start another child support case and go through another twenty-one years of terror. I'd recently learned that New York State raised the age from 18 to 21, meaning that you're obligated to take care of the child until 21 no matter what. Most fathers, like me, thought that once the child was 18, you were free. No-no-no! It's 21, or 26 if the child is ambitious and goes to college.

When Tracy and I get back around the block, I give her a couple of dollars to get her kids some food and she goes upstairs. I now have to muster up some more courage to complete this mission. I go get the carton of cigarettes and go home. When I get to my apartment, I do the usual and check the mail on the table, then I walk into the living room and see that my momma has fallen asleep again on the couch while watching television. I stand there and watch her sleep soundly and wonder what kind of ass-whipping she would put on me if she knew what I was about to do. I shake my head to myself, remembering how happy I was and how happy and proud she was when I first got this job. Now it has come to this, me smuggling in cigarettes to an inmate, even though I know and trust him, to get myself out of a dick dilemma. I know that she would not approve, but as a man, sometimes to keep things straight you have to do what you have to do. I go to my room and this time there is no dancing, no music, and no drinking. It's me, my conscience, and a carton of Newport cigarettes.

I'm nervous as hell and very paranoid on my way to work the next day. I'm on the bus looking everyone in the face, wondering if I am being followed. I have this guilty feeling that everyone knows what I am about to do. I get to work and I am at the main control building waiting for the route bus to take me to my jail. While I am waiting there I see some senior officers that I normally joke around with in the morning. I know that they are going to start in on me about me always being a new jack to them no matter how much time on the job I accumulated. Well, this morning I am not in the mood for that or anything else, so when they start in on me and have everybody on the bus cracking up laughing, I blurt out to one of them, "Muthafucka, are you still beating your wife!?" Dead silence. Game, set, match. Everybody on the bus looks at me in shock, because we all know that it is true, but I guess they feel like what the hell is wrong with me and that I do not have to put it out on front street like that. I give him a sarcastic smile and say, "Have a good day!" Then I get off the bus and go to my jail. That little episode reduces my stress level for just a few seconds. Now I am standing in line about to enter my jail with a carton of cigarettes tucked into the side of my pants.

I purposely wore my uniform to work today so that when I beeped going through the metal detector it wouldn't be a problem. Here we go. My breathing gets louder. My heart rate increases. When it is time for me to pass through, the captain who is standing there to oversee the search process stops me. *Shit! I knew it was too good to be true. I'm caught.* He then yells to the other officers behind me, "Now see, this is what I am talking about, an officer that comes to work already dressed and ready to start the day." He then pats me on my back as I walk through beeping. I didn't waste any time going to my locker. I go straight to roll call because all I want to do is get these things off me.

I'm standing at roll call listening to the announcements of the day. They're taking longer than usual. I look around at the other officers because I swear that everybody knows what I am doing. After we're dismissed I go straight to my post, no joking around, no staff kitchen, no nothing, just straight to my post so that I can take my count, relieve the midnight officer, and take care of my business. I get to my post and make a tour, which is nothing more than counting how many bodies are in cells. I get to Flocko's cell and he is already up and on his door. I wink as I go by and he nods. I tell the midnight officer, "Full house." Then I sign the count slip that verifies this and the officer is out the door. When he leaves, I lock the gate behind him and now I am alone because my partner, the B officer, has to go to the morning search and won't report to post until it's done. I quickly crack Flocko's cell and he comes out talking loud, asking me to open the broom closet because he and I know that morning, noon, and night there is always another inmate watching everything that goes down. I start to talk loud, telling him what I want cleaned and as he steps inside the utility closet I wipe off the carton with a wet napkin then hand it to him, leaving no fingerprints of mine on it. He puts it under his shirt, picks up the equipment, and goes back to his cell. He knows that if for some reason the search comes now and he gets caught, it's his loss. The rest of the day I was a nervous wreck, and every time someone yelled "On the gate!" so that I could let them in my area, I would get a surge of anxiety, thinking it was the authorities coming to get me.

When I got home and retrieved my mail off the table I went to my room. I lay on my bed and thought about what I had done. The whole thing, from the abortion to the move with Flocko. I was also sipping, and it felt good. The stress and the paranoia had gone, because I pulled it off and no one jumped out from behind my bed to bust me. I went through my mail and saw nothing but bills, and guess what—I had the money to pay them.

CHAPTER 26

THE ORGANIZATION

"Forty-seven, forty-eight, forty-nine, fifty . . ."

I was counting out the number of Top tobacco pouches and stuffing them inside my stab-proof vest. The pouches were bulky under my vest, but I'm a heavyset guy, so it was the perfect cover-up. Every officer had to wear one, too.

Going through the front entrance was a breeze, because it was a post no one wanted. It was the most tedious and was more repetitious than manning a housing area. At least in a housing area an officer could relax a little and maybe get some sleep if needed. Not on the front entrance post. You had cameras watching you, people coming back and forth all day. From start to finish there was no time to rest. If officers were permanently assigned to the front entrance, most likely they were only half-ass doing their job because they were upset that they had to work that post all day. Sometimes I was able to go through just by listening and empathizing with the officer that was bitching about the post.

Flocko and I had been rocking for a minute. Cigarettes and tobacco were in high demand due to a recent ban by Mayor Mike Bloomberg. I was making money and slowly getting my life back. Although I was still going back and forth trying to get an adjustment on my child support payment. Every time I would end up with the same judge and the same results. The last time I was in court, I managed to put a little smile on my face after the judge shat on me, because I knew my bills were getting paid on time and I had money in my pocket.

Flocko was my first lieutenant. He had recruited some loyal workers that did most of the dirty work for us. I was cautious about who he dealt with. I did a background check on them by looking at their charges and talking to other inmates that might know them from the streets. I wanted to make sure that they were here for the reason that they said they were.

The profit from the cigarette trade in jail outweighs that of any drug hustle on the street. For one two-dollar pouch of Top tobacco you can make two hundred to three hundred dollars, depending on how desperate some of these inmates are for a smoke. And don't get an inmate who just came into the system and has been smoking all his life—he's a cash cow as long as his people support him from the outside. I was amazed when Flocko brought back cash to me from inside the jail. *How the hell do these inmates get so much cash inside the jail?* Flocko explained to me one day that money like that comes straight from the visitors' floor and that very seldom can you slip it through the mailroom.

Most of the money is made on Wednesdays, visitors' day. There are no visitations on Mondays and Tuesdays. Inmates would get straight cash on the visitors' floor as if it was out of an ATM. I wore gloves for when the cash would reach me. One could only guess how it got transported.

We had our ways to limit suspicion of who was distributing tobacco. We never distributed a large amount at one time, nor did we sell or make sales on Mondays and Tuesdays, the no-visitation days.

And most transactions went down either at recreation or when they went to eat and there was no way officers could watch all the inmates all the time. The officers were outnumbered twenty to one. This was also why nothing could be done about fights or slashings until after the fact. If a riot broke out in the mess hall while inmates were feeding and the officers were locked in there with the inmates, the best they could do was contain the situation to one area. Flocko also never carried a large amount on his person and often broke the pouch down into little cigarettes called rollies. If there was a drought, Flocko could sell rollies for upward of twenty dollars each, or he'd sometimes trade rollies for an inmate's commissary.

So far, so good. I would deliver the pouches and by the end of the day I would have my money. Days went by smoothly. There were no incidents to report. Flocko, being a general in one of the many Spanish gangs in the jail, helped keep things going smoothly. I could never keep track of what inmate held what rank due to the high rate of turnover. Each individual had a different case and different charges. I'd finish my tour and jet home to get some much-needed sleep.

One day I arrived at my projects via city bus and taxicab. I ran into my mother coming from the corner store. She had groceries in her hands and just handed them to me before she said a word. Then she began to speak as we made our way to our building, walking through the graveyard. (The graveyard was a path we had to pass along the way that's littered with makeshift memorials with pictures of young people in their prime at parties or posing when they were at their best with nice clothes on, and you know that there were half a dozen liquor bottles and candles that were posted up in front of the pictures, I guess to show that people celebrated this or that individual's life.) My mother seemed unfazed by all the death that was around us. I guess her age and the number of years that we've been living here have made her numb to senseless deaths. When we walk into the lobby the elevator was about to close, so I ran and caught the door and held it until my mother caught up and got on. I knew that somebody was on it already but did not look to see who it was before grabbing the door.

When my mother stepped into the elevator I heard a familiar voice say, "Hey, girl, where you been?" And when I looked it was Ms. Daniels, and by her side stood Biz. Our eyes locked. I was a little shocked, because I had not seen him since the incident in jail and did not know that he had come home. His eyes were ice-cold and unmoved by my presence. I saw that the wounds on his face had healed. Obviously he had not told his mother what had happened, because they were chatting away as the door closed and the elevator took off. They were going on about the happenings in church this past Sunday, mentioning Pastor Johnson's toupee coming off during singing rehearsals and that Deacon Jones was messing with one of the ushers.

All the while me and Biz never said a word to each other and remained staring at one another. I saw that he had the grill face on, so I matched his intensity. At the time I had not known that it was him under that hoodie and that my job was at stake. I knew that trying to explain that to him was futile, so I didn't even try. Then he made a move and lifted up his shirt, exposing a snub-nosed .38. I was caught off guard by this. Then I looked at him, then at our mothers, who were oblivious to what was happening. The fact that he couldn't care less that our mothers were there angered me, so at that point I gave him an evil glare and zipped down the jacket that I had on and pulled it to the side to expose my 9 mm Smith and muthafuckin' Wesson. This time I looked at him, then at my mother, then back at him, silently indicating, *I'll shoot you and take a bullet before you harm her.* Then I unclipped the holster that secured my weapon. He saw the look on my face, a look that I know he knew from when we were kids growing up. With that, he decided to make the best move he could make for the both of us and put his shirt back down, indicating to me another time and another place. I was undeterred by his move and kept my hand on my gun, letting him know, *I will be ready at all times, Negro.* The elevator stopped, and as they got off, Ms. Daniels said bye to my mother and looked at me and winked.

"Take it easy, Ms. Daniels," I said.

"Bye, Ms. Heyward," Biz said, and got off the elevator.

The door closed and my moms turned and looked at me. I looked at her and wondered if she had a clue as to what just happened. Then out of nowhere, she took her thumb, licked it, and wiped something off that I had on the side of my face.

CHAPTER 27

DIRTY TACTICS

"THAT BITCH CAN SUCK MY DICK IN MACY'S WINDOW AT CHRISTMAS!" an inmate screams at a female officer as I approach my housing area for my morning shift.

When I get on my post, the B officer informs me that the inmate arrived last night from another jail after getting into an altercation there. I'm dirty with pouches of tobacco, so I have to think fast and find a way to hide my product. So I tell him to go ahead and do the search, and that I'll handle the inmate that's screaming. The B officer is more than happy to leave, telling me on his way out that that bitch, meaning the A officer from the midnight shift, is nothing but trouble. I nod and let him out of the area. Then as soon as he's gone I stash my stuff and proceed down the walkway to see how my day is going to start.

As I'm walking down the walkway toward the female officer, who's standing in front of an inmate's cell, I pass Flocko's cell. He tells me through his door that that's some new troublemaking nigga that came in last night. I continue walking, getting close to the officer, and she turns and sees me coming. Then, all of a sudden, she begins getting really disrespectful with the inmate, telling him he is a bum nigga for being in jail and how some other man is butt-fucking his girl right now, and so on. When I get to the inmate's cell he comes back at her raw, saying, "Bitch, you better respect J-Murder, you ugly fat bucktooth orangutan-in-the-face-looking bitch! Look atcha self. I wouldn't fuck you right now if you begged me, and I've been down some joints. You know you ain't no dime on the streets. Hell, you ain't even average! Don't let these niggas in here fool you into thinking you're somebody, 'cause you're not. They just trying to get their dick sucked! You're just a thirsty ass cock-gazing bitch, always creeping up on a nigga when he gets out the shower trying to get a peek. You ain't getting no dick in the streets but walk around here like you the Queen of Sheba or something."

I'm about to step in and shut him down when I look at her and see that she is teary eyed. I'm at a loss for words. *Come on, sis, even if he's right you're not supposed to let him see you like this.* He sees that he has her stuck and starts to laugh out loud and says, "Don't worry, bitch. I'm a nice guy. I'll let you lick it later on when nobody's around." Then he steps back and exposes himself. As I step toward his cell, she pulls me back and says, "Heyward, I fight my own battles," and gestures for me to follow her. I do so and we go back to the officers' station. When we get there she pulls out the inmate's locator card with all his information on it, like his home address and what charges he is in for, and so on. Puzzled, I ask her what she is doing, and she responds, "Just sit back, and learn something. Everything can't be handled with brawn. You have to use your head sometimes, especially us females."

She makes a phone call and gets the inmate's PIN number that identifies him whenever he goes to commissary or uses the telephone. Once she gets this she calls around to other areas in the jail and tells the other officers to give it out to other inmates so that they can use the money in the inmate's account, thus leaving Mr.

Loud and Disrespectful high and dry with no money and unable to make phone calls. Inside, everybody knows that being able to call home keeps an inmate sane sometimes. When he finds out what has happened to him there will be nothing that he can do. I often wonder why some inmates think that they can say or do things to a CO when the CO always has the last laugh and can do just about anything while they're locked up in here. She hangs up, looks over at me, and says, "I ain't finished." Then she calls our area supervisor and says that we have one who wants to sign in. At the same time, she reaches inside the front desk, pulling out an inmate sign-in form that states, "I am a homosexual and want to go to homosexual housing for protection." She fills it out with his information on it and signs his name to it. She then tells me that she's cool with the captain, and after she tells him that the inmate exposed himself to her he will do this for her, which means that Mr. Peep Show will be forced to go and live in a housing area that houses only gay inmates. Mind you, she is doing all this when she should be on her way home. Hell hath no fury like a woman scorned. She leaves with the papers in hand that are going to change this inmate's life forever.

When she's gone, I unlock Flocko's cell and he immediately comes to ask me if I want him to take care of this fool. I tell him no, because it's already been taken care of. By midday our business is going smooth as usual, then I hear my supervisor yell, "On the gate!" I open the gate to see the captain enter with two other "come-walk-with-mes." When I see this I know that the fix is in and they are here to aid the captain with the transfer of the rude inmate, a transfer where there will be resistance. I unlock the troublemaker's cell and give the captain his locator card. When the inmate comes up the walkway I hear him bragging to the other inmates, telling them that he's a handful and that he's no walk in the park. Then he asks me where he is going. I just look at him as if I am giving him his last rites. Then with a cocky attitude he says, "It don't matter because I am going to eat wherever I go." He then looks at the captain and the hired help and yells back to the other inmates in the area, "Y'all see how they have to come get me! They got the whole goon squad out here for ya boy!" Then he laughs, picks up his bags, and tells the captain, "Let's go!"

They leave and I go to adjust my books, subtracting the inmate off my total count. Suddenly I hear, "CO! CO! On the gate!" I get up to see what's going on, thinking that the inmate must have found out where he is heading and decided to put up a fight. I run to my gate and open it, ready to assist, when I see that it is not my inmate that was yelling. It is another inmate trying to get in the housing area across the hall from mine. The crazy thing is that he is covered in blood from his shirt to his pants. He jerks on the bars frantically, all the while looking over his shoulder like he is running from someone. I thought that he had gotten jumped by some inmates and that they were in hot pursuit.

Another officer comes to the gate and sees the inmate is covered in blood and decides not to let him in because he does not know what is going on. Whatever happened went bad. Then another captain and some officers come running out of a nearby exit and tackle the inmate to the ground and put cuffs on him. Then they apply the "pounce and drag technique" to his ass all the way down the hall. I'm curious as to what happened. Then I get a call from the main control room for me to lock my inmates back in because the jail is going on lockdown. I ask the frantic officer on the other end what had happened and she says, "An inmate was just killed in the housing area where Officer Bryant was working."

CHAPTER 28

TACTICAL SEARCH OPERATION

"On the gate!" a captain from another jail calls out to me so I can open it for him and his search team.

Due to the murder that had occurred we were now having a TSO (tactical search operation). That's when officers from one jail get to visit another jail and catch up with officers that they have not seen in a long time. Oh, and they come to wreak havoc and search the jail, too. It's a joint effort to search the entire jail, to shake up the inmates and to let them know that we are not going to tolerate this kind of behavior.

I open the gate. I'm not stressing, because I made Flocko give me all the pouches so that I could put them where I know TSO won't search—in my jacket or in the officers' station. I see a few familiar faces. They nod to me. I nod back as they go and line up in front of the inmates' cells. The men come in first while the females stay outside and wait. The men have to respectfully and professionally strip-search the male inmates. As I crack open the cells all you hear is officers giving the inmates orders politely. "Strip, muthafucka! Hand me your clothing one piece at a time and don't shake shit out because if you fling anything my way you got a problem." After the clothing is searched comes the most embarrassing and humiliating part for the inmate, the cavity search. An officer orders an inmate to "open ya cocksucker [mouth] and stick out ya ball licker [tongue]." The officer says to another officer, "Half these punks are fags anyway." The officer checks to see if an inmate has any weapons such as razors hiding in his mouth. An inmate has been known to hide as many as twenty-two razors in his mouth, effectively eating and chewing with no problem. Then it's, "Let me see ya dick beaters [hands]."

"Wiggle the muthafuckas!"

"Putcha hands up; let me see ya funky underarms."

"Now turn around and bend over and spread ya aasssss cheeks!"

"Let me see if you're a lover [been having anal sex] or a fighter [been keeping the wolves up off ya]."

This maneuver is to see if an inmate has a weapon hiding in his butt. You'd be surprised at what you would find in an inmate's ass. Some of these guys are used as mules to transport weapons and drugs around the jail. I got to give it to them because it takes a lot of discipline to walk around with stuff in your butt like that. Inmates do this on the regular because in some cases they may have beef with a lot of inmates throughout the prison system and have to keep a weapon in their ass at all times. This is another very important reason not to ever come to jail. You don't want to have to learn ass control 101 in order to save your ass.

After all that, the inmate is instructed to get dressed and step outside his cell carrying his mattress. I know that this search is going to be ugly and provoking. ESU (Emergency Service Unit), or the goon squad, as the inmates call it, is on standby for any inmate that felt like he was a grown ass man and did not have to be subjected to this type of treatment. At this time the females enter and it's a joint effort to destroy everything from pictures to sacred items—I mean everything. The inmates are instructed to raise their hands to speak to a captain if they have any questions about how an officer is tossing their cell. A hand goes up and the captain says, "Putcha fuckin' hand down. I don't want to hear shit." The inmate yells, "But, Captain, that's my legal work. It took me six months to get it all together to prove my innocence and I have court tomorrow." The captain responds by yelling, "Extraction!" This lets the ESU know that there is a disorderly inmate who needs to be removed from the area.

When they move in, the inmate continues to plead his case. They try to cuff him. He starts to fight like he's fighting for his life, yelling, "I just didn't want her to destroy my legal paperwork." At the same time the female officer throws the papers in the middle of the floor among some other items and pours a container of milk over them and keeps it moving as he is beaten and dragged out of the area.

While the search is happening, officers begin to question what happened.

"I heard an inmate got murdered," one female officer tells another while still carrying out the search process.

"Yeah, and the inmate who did it did not belong inside that housing area," another officer responds while throwing the contents of an inmate's cell out into the corridor.

"How the fuck did that happen?" the other officer asks.

Then a captain walks up and joins the conversation.

"It looks like a hit of some sort was carried out."

The other officer's eyebrows go up and he asks, "How did an inmate from another housing area get inside an area where he doesn't belong to kill another inmate?"

"I got one better than that. The only reason the murderer got caught was because he could not get inside his own housing area after he committed the murder. So not only did he get in but how did he get out without anybody seeing him?" says the captain.

"Ain't we suppose to search the inmates every time they exit and enter a housing area?" an officer asks.

"Tah, what officer you know does that?"

CHAPTER 29

JUICY FRUITS

"Five, six, seven, eight, and pivot and half step and half step. Come on, girl, you have to move your hips!" says one inmate to another.

The jail was on lockdown for a couple of days after the killing and there was little to no movement throughout the jail. That made it hard for me and Flocko to get money. So I decided to stay for overtime, which landed me in homosexual housing. I'm sitting there as the B officer, being forced to watch a jail rendition of "Rip the Runway." These inmates are placed in here for their own safety and for the good of the jail. Mainly, we segregate the homosexuals one, so that they will not be abused and raped repeatedly, and two, so that the in-the-closet homo thugs won't be fighting each other over who is going to wife one of them. It helps to keep the jail calm, so to speak. So I was sitting there while Gerald Davis, aka Geraldine, and Sam Brown, aka Shelly, practiced for a show where they are planning to perform. For who and where, I have no idea, nor do I give a damn. Gay or not, they're just inmates to me.

While I was sitting there, an inmate by the name of Briggs approached me. He stood across from me and began talking, more like pleading his case, telling me that just because he's in this housing area doesn't mean he's gay. I just nodded like, *Ooookay*. Then he continued to explain that he signed in here just to stay in the building so that he wouldn't be transferred again. I nodded, not really giving a fuck. Then another inmate, seeing that I was approachable to talk to, joined the conversation to give his résumé. His approach to homosexual housing was totally opposite. He said, "Heyward, I just got sentenced to double life for a body and I ain't never gonna see the streets again. My gun game in the streets is no joke and I suck a mean dick."

Check, please!

He continued, while looking into the TV room at the other inmates, "I gives a fuck about what somebody in the streets think of me? If any of these younguns come in here, I'm taking it. Sheeit, I got a ripe one already. He fought it when he first got here but I broke him and now we're in love." I just gave him a look like, "Oh, yeah," and at that moment the A officer yelled out for me to take a count. *Thank you, Jesus.* I yelled out for all the inmates to stand still where they were so I could get an accurate count without doing it the right way and having them go stand by their cells. I counted all the ones in the dayroom, then proceeded to walk down the tier, looking inside each cell to count the inmates inside. I made a round and came back to the window of the A station and told her my count and she shook her head, saying that I was off by one. I took another count of the inmates in the dayroom, then went back down the tier to count again, but this time slowly. I was halfway done when I looked inside this one particular cell and saw a bed empty but little drops of what appeared to be blood on the floor. I yelled for the officer to electronically open the cell and she did.

When I went inside I noticed a trickle of blood coming from under the bed to where I saw the drops. I went to the bed and lifted the blanket up and was stunned at what I saw. There was an inmate under the bed wrapped from head to toe in a sheet with nothing exposed but his buttocks, which had blood dripping from them. I also saw that something was lightly cut into his skin, but I could not make out what it was. I panicked and frantically dragged him from under the bed, hoping that he wasn't dead. I heard him moan, which was a relief. Then I rolled him over and noticed that his whole head was wrapped, with just his mouth exposed. I could see dried-up semen all around his mouth and I could only imagine what they used him for. I knew also the amount of trouble that I along with the other officer were going to be in if we could not come up with some answers for how we allowed this to happen.

I slowly unwrapped his head so I could get a look at his face and he started trembling and sobbing at the same time. I think that he thought that I was one of his attackers coming back to do him more harm. When I finally finished unwrapping his head, he looked at me and I just turned away and shook my head. I couldn't look him in the face because it was the loudmouth kid that had invited the female CO to see his private parts the other day. He began to loosen his arms so that he could finish unwrapping himself. I walked out into the hall and leaned against the wall while he got himself together.

The A officer yelled out to me, "What's up? Is there something wrong?" I told her I found the one on the count that I had missed. I stood there contemplating my next move, trying to figure out how I, the B officer, allowed this to happen when I was supposed to make a tour of the area every hour so things like this wouldn't happen. I didn't know what to feel right then because I was not directly responsible for him being here but I did nothing to stop it either. Was he a kid who a couple of months ago was out in the city running around disrespecting his moms by not going to school, by not work-ing, smoking blunts all day, being with the wrong crowd, and deal-ing drugs? Or was he just a good kid with good parents raised in a good home that just got caught up at the wrong place at the wrong time due to peer pressure from his friends? I felt that a lot of these young men that come through here really think that jail is some kind of badge of honor and really don't realize that they are in here with people that have been transformed to individuals that no longer live by society's rules. I know that whatever the case was with him, he never thought that he would end up like this.

"Heyward." He called my name and I came to the front of his cell.

Now he was dressed and lying on his bed in a fetal position fac-ing the wall so that I could not see his face. I told him that I was going to call the clinic and get him some medical attention.

"No, please just get me out of here. I don't want to go to the clinic because then everybody will know what happened to me and I can't be in here with that out around the jail," he said.

"Okay," I said, and went to the officers' station to fill out a sign-out form for him, stating that he was no longer gay and did not want to stay in this housing area.

I explained briefly what happened to the A officer, and she was more than happy to get him the hell up out of her area, wanting no part of his situation to fall on her.

Moments later, the captain arrived, and I personally escorted the inmate out of his cell and out of the area. He had his head down and his belongings in a bag draped over his shoulders. Gone was the young vibrant loudmouth gangster from the other day. Gone was the disrespectful penis-flashing individual and gone altogether was the gang-banging, I-can-live-anywhere thug known as J-Murder. In his place was a different person, someone who would probably have mental problems and nightmares for years to come from what he'd just suffered. From now on J-Murder, aka Jamal Thomas, would assume a new name. He would be called "Juicy Fruits" by certain individuals. The reason I know this is that it was carved in his back for bend-over purposes—right above his butt cheeks.

CHAPTER 30

BIZ IS BACK

After leaving the little shop of horrors, a Negro was tired. I felt that they had gotten their five dollars' worth of work out of me that day. So I made a beeline to the liquor store, then to Bryant's house. When I got there, Officer Z. Jones, another one of the three amigos, was there. She opened the door for me and gave me a look like, "She's in bad shape," referring to Bryant. When I went inside I saw Bryant sitting on a couch located in her kitchen, clutching a bottle of vodka. She looked up at me and I could tell that she had been crying.

"Get a cup, muthafucka," she says.

"I already do," I tell her, and open the bottle of Hennessy that I bought and was about to drink, when Jones yells at me.

"Neanderthal, get a cup with some ice. Nobody's going to be drinking behind you!" she explains.

Then she climbs over the couch, which actually separates the kitchen from the living room, and goes into the fridge. She yells, "Girl, you don't have any more ice?" Bryant gets up, opens her hall closet that has a deep freezer and an illegal clothes dryer in it—the kind you're not supposed to have in the projects. She grabs two metal ice trays by their handles and slams them onto the table, then she grabs my Hennessy bottle right out of my hand and takes it to the head while she looks over at Jones as if to say, "You the only bitch worrying about ice." Then she flops down on the couch and starts crying. While sobbing she says, "Them muthafuckas trying to take my job! I got kids. How are they going to put this shit all on me?"

"What are you talking about? What happened?" Jones asks.

"Check it, I come to the post and the gate was opened with inmates leaving out going to different services. I walk into the bubble where King and Fran are both sitting in there talking. King was supposed to be on the floor watching the inmates. They know that I'm the meal relief, so I ask them which one of them is going to meal first. Then I hear an inmate yelling, 'CO! CO! Open the gate!' I look up and I see some inmates scrambling to their cells and some others standing there staring at this inmate on the door who is trying to get out. I buzz the door so he can get out and he stumbles out and collapses, holding his stomach with blood all over him. I run to his side while Fran called the clinic, and far as I know, King is locking the inmates down so that no one goes anyplace. I am on my knees next to the inmate and . . ." Bryant pauses, weeping uncontrollably, with tears coming down heavily on her face.

When she finally looks up at us, it's as if she doesn't remember we're there. Then she quickly gathers herself together and continues.

"I'm kneeling there . . ." she says, ". . . and the inmate is looking at me and breathing heavy. He's holding his stomach and, Heyward, you could just see the blood gushing out all over the floor from his wound."

She begins to weep again but still continues to talk. "He reached up and I grabbed his hand and that was the first time I saw that he had a big hole in his stomach, and the blood. Heyward, the blood just kept pouring out of him! I grabbed his T-shirt that was almost ripped off of him and tried to put it over his wound. I took his hand

and put it over his wound and told him to hold it there. He did it but you could tell that he did not have the strength to apply any pressure. So I did it for him. We were there with the inmate waiting for the clinic staff to arrive. I mean seconds seemed like minutes and minutes seemed like hours before they came. So I am holding his hand and as I look around I see that now he and I are in a puddle of his blood. His breathing is slowing down and he's looking at me, then he whispered to me because he could not talk and said, 'CO, please don't let me die,' then his eyes rolled up, his grip loosens on my hand, and I knew that he was gone."

Now she's all-out bawling and Jones goes over and puts Bryant's head on her shoulder and hugs her. My stupid ass is sitting there dumbfounded and not knowing what I could do to comfort her, so I lift the bottle up and drink some more. She stops crying, wipes her face, and grabs her bottle of vodka. Before she can drink it, Jones tries to take it from her, saying that she doesn't need any more. Ya know she gave her the if-you-don't-let-go-of-this-bottle look. Bryant took a drink and then said, "Now these muthafucka are asking me questions like 'Why I let the inmate in?' 'How did I let him out of the area without Fran and King seeing him?' I told them that they're crazy. That I did not see an inmate come or go! Shit, I didn't even know that they caught him until they told me later. I thought that the inmate that did it was from the same housing area. They telling me shit like I am going to lose my job, that I could face criminal charges and all that." She breaks down again and starts whining, "What am I going to do? I had nothing to do with this shit. Why are they trying to pin it all on me?" Jones and I just look at each other because we have no answers for her.

—

I hopped in a cab and went home. While walking to my building everything that Bryant had said was running through my head. There were so many questions and scenarios that were going on with this situation, like why were they trying to blame only Bryant? There were three officers on that post, so could one of them have let the inmate in the area unauthorized? Or worse, did they know that he was going to attack another inmate and allow it to happen? I shook my head and thought to myself, *People are getting killed because of officers doing illegal shit but I am not the one to throw stones because as it is my black ass is bringing in pouches of tobacco.*

Just then I heard *POW! POW!* Gunshots. The rounds were hitting the wall by me just above my head. *Oh, shit, someone is shooting at me!* I pulled out my gun, then dropped and crawled behind a nearby car. I waited a second and looked up just in time to see a figure running away and guess what, he had a hoodie on. I recognized the hoodie, because the last time I saw it was when I broke his face. I'm stunned and outraged because I can't believe what just happened. After growing up together and all the shit we went through together as kids, tonight Biz just tried to kill me.

CHAPTER 31

HANDLE YA BUSINESS

The next day I'm on my way to work, still a little rattled about Biz shooting at me the night before. Biz needed to be dealt with and soon. I wasn't trying to be in a situation where I'm always having to watch my back—in my own neighborhood. I think about visiting his moms about the whole thing but change my mind because she didn't have anything to do with what happened. And Biz probably wasn't staying with her anyway.

I arrive at work, approaching the entrance to my jail, when I see that there is a gung-ho captain searching officers as they enter. I'm not worried because by now I've done this a dozen times and I know to be fully dressed in my officer's uniform when I am making a drop. There is a female in front of me who's complaining about her rights as an officer being violated and threatening to call the union because the captain has asked her to open her bag. I know better than to bring one, because it slows down the process. She opens her bag and sarcastically says, "Take a look!" It almost sounds like a dare. I am close to her and the captain because I'm next and I also get to see the contents of her bag. The captain looks and then jumps back and so do I. In her bag was a jelly doughnut, aka a used Kotex. The female officer just stands there with a smirk on her face and asks, "Can I go now?" The captain nods, appearing a little embarrassed. I chuckle, because sometimes you just can't make this shit up.

After that, all the by-the-book precision searching stops and it is back to business as usual with us just being able to put our bags through the scanning machine and keep it moving, beeping and all. I make my way to roll call and prepare for inspection. We do this dance every morning. The captains come and inspect our equipment, which consists of a flashlight, a 911, which is a sharpened knife curled at the end so that we can cut an inmate down if he is trying to hang himself, also a pen holder and pens so there is no excuse for not being able to write reports and do your paperwork, and a memo pad. The pad is for you to be able to write a mini journal of what you did on that day. It's supposed to be a legal document in case you're called to court and have to testify on what you did.

The captains make their way through the ranks inspecting officers. You see various levels of equipment being presented. There are some senior officers who ain't writing shit and who ain't cutting an inmate down. They will show the captain a rusty memo book with rubber bands around it to keep it together and toilet paper on the inside. Mind you, the captains are supposed to sign the, ah, toilet paper indicating that it was inspected that day. The 911 knife is supposed to have a serial number on it, and if you lose it you're supposed to be in really big trouble. I guess the captains know which officers give a shit about being written up and which ones don't. So sometimes they don't even bother enforcing anything with said individuals.

This time the warden decides to show up to the roll call, taking time to mingle among us common folk. He starts giving us a speech. "These inmates are not your friends." *You mean Flocko?* He says, "They will give you up in a heartbeat."

Some heartbeat, because I know Flocko has been loyal. He continues, "There is nothing that they can do for you." *Well, that ain't exactly true.* "So don't get caught up." *I won't, but good looking out anyway.*

After roll call I go to my post and am greeted by a female officer named Rains. I am still on edge a bit but begin to feel better because we were cool and I was probably going to have a good day. Sometimes you can have a fucked-up day if you get with a by-the-book type of officer. Me and Rains often flirted but never had sex. We would talk a lot of times and I could tell that in the streets she was a down-for-whatever type of female. I even met her boyfriend once, who happened to be big in the drug game. When I step inside the officers' station she says, "What's up, money bags?" I say, "What's up?" but just look at her like, "You got the wrong person with the money bags name." She is the B officer from the midnight tour and is supposed to go to the search. She is one of the officers who hate the search and never went when she was supposed to. So now I have a problem because I want to hit Flocko off with some pouches. Due to the recent murder, things had been tight in the jail and the money was slow. Now I'm accustomed to getting my money every time I come to work and I need it right now because I started gambling again and the addiction had me open. I want to get her off this post so that I can take care of business. Then she says, "Go ahead, money bags, do what you have to do. You know I'm good."

Confused, I look at her, puzzled, and ask, "What are you talking about?" She smiles and says, "Breathe easy, Big Hey, I just want to let you know a few things. I did not have this post last night. I had the captain switch the post I had so I could be with you this morning." I raise my eyebrows because now I am really fucked up. She says, "And I know everything." I still stick to my guns and look at her with the I-still-don't-know-what-you're-talking-about face. She then breaks down my whole organization without stopping for me to either agree or deny her allegations, and after she finishes, without me saying a word, she gets up and pops open Flocko's cell.

I'm stuck.

I don't know how to react right now.

I'm scared.

I'm angry because she knows so much. I am wondering how she got her information. I'm wondering who else knows and all that. I try to hide how I'm feeling right now by doing my best impression of a blank face. She sits back down, pulls out a fingernail file, and says, "Like I said before, handle ya business."

Flocko comes up to the officers' station to see that we have company. I see something in his expression when he looks at Rains that suggests he knows her. He stops looking at her, then he looks at me, confused, like, "I know you're not going to do anything in front of her." I tell him that I need to holla at him in the inmate TV room. I buzz the door and go in while Rains sits back and continues to file her fingernails. I pull him to the side and with a serious face I ask him if he knows her.

"I know of her," he says.

"What do you mean by that?" I ask.

"My people told me before that she was going around giving head for cash," Flocko says.

"What!?" I ask.

"Yeah, word is that she is a cokehead and is giving up head and ass for cash. I never had her but some of my peeps did. At first I didn't believe them because you know how niggas in here be lying on their dick, but when more than one inmate says the same thing . . ."

He throws his hands up and shrugs as if to say, "Hey, you never know." But what I really need to know is how did she find out about me. I tell him everything that she knows, right down to the part of her popping him out of his cell. He has the look of guilt on his face like somebody fucked up. Then he swears to me that it wasn't him and suggests that it may have been one of his workers. I could tell that he was telling the truth because he now had the worried look that this might fuck up the joint business venture that we had going. I tell him to find out on his end and I will find out from her. He went back to his cell and I went to the officers' bathroom. Once inside I'm thinking that I have to figure this shit out. One thing I know for sure, she ain't here to rat me out. She wants something from me. I had to find out. I had to confront the situation.

I go back to the officers' station and I sit down in a chair directly across from her and I say, "Okay, shoot, let me know what's up." She turns her chair toward me, leans back to where I can see the imprint of her coochie lips through her tight pants, and pats it with her hand. I feel that Flocko was telling the truth about her and then she starts to explain. She says, "Hey, we have been cool for a minute and I feel that I can trust you with what I am about to tell you." I give her a look like, "I am all ears." Then she says, "I found out about you through one of my customers who is locked up in here."

"Customers?" I ask. "What, are you dropping pouches, too?"

"No disrespect," she looks at me and says, "but I couldn't pay my mortgage with pouch money. You know that they bagged my baby [her boyfriend] a couple of months ago and shit started getting real tight as far as the money goes. He was paying for mostly everything and I was banking mine but now I have to keep shit right for my four little girls and keep money on his commissary. That's why I've been doing me."

While she's talking, I start letting the inmates out of their cells to start the day. She continues, "I started with a few officers in here that have been all up in my face trying to sex me. They were always offering to buy me things and take me on trips and all that. So I just converted all that shit into cash. The first one, I just told him that I needed a bill paid and he did it for a two-minute slurp session." She makes a slurp sound with her mouth and says, "Right there in area two top. And after that I never looked back.

"Honestly speaking, most of these chicks around here are giving it up for free, and besides me I know of only two others that are rocking like me, but they are bum bitches and be settling for mink coats and snakeskin boots. A chick like me is making school tuition and mortgage money," she says.

I ask her how she found out about me. She leans back again so that I can see her cunt lips through her pants and pops it twice, then says, "You'd be surprised at what a man will say and do once a woman tightens up on him. It took a few times, but an inmate by the name of Moe told me about Flocko always having tobacco and never running out even when it ain't visits. So I sat back and watched until I found out he was here in eight upper. Then, judging from the conversations that miraculously we don't have anymore about your child support situation, I put two and two together and here I am."

"What do you want?" I ask. "I mean, obviously you ain't ratting me out, so you must want something."

"On the real," she said, "I need protection and I feel as cool as we are and what you're into and what I am into that I can only trust you."

"Protection from who? Officers? Inmates?"

"More like a lookout with the officers," she said, "because I am about to fuck with some bigwigs and I just want you to know who they are just in case a bitch gets into some real trouble, which I doubt, but you never know."

"What's in it for me?"

She pops her cooch again.

"I got enough of that," I tell her.

"I can move pouches for you, one hand washes the other," she says.

I know she can move and get into places that Flocko couldn't, and if shit hit the fan, I wouldn't get caught unless I got caught dirty with pouches on me; everything else would be hearsay. *Can I really trust her?* Then I rationalize, *Hello, you are fucking with a team of inmates, so an officer selling ass might be your safest bet.*

I look at her for a long minute and she looks back at me as if she is scared and is wondering has she made a mistake about me. "It's on," I say. And seeing that her antics have me harder than a roll of quarters, I ask her when I can sample the merchandise.

"As soon as you can lock these muthafuckas in," she says.

CHAPTER 32

OVERTIME

"That's a man! That bitch is a man!" inmates are shouting at the television.

I have gotten stuck on overtime again. I'm working the Mental Observation housing area, aka the Nut House. I'm sitting in the dayroom watching a bunch of inmates watch a talk show that wants the audience to guess whether the person standing onstage is a man or woman. The inmates scream out their guess again, "That bitch is a man!" Another inmate screams out, "If it is, I'd still fuck her shiiieet!" Then they all slap each other a high five while laughing out loud. The MO house is where people are either crazy or pretending to be crazy to try and beat their case. Right now these fools are jumping off the wall until they hear their favorite call, which is MEDICATION! *Ah, right on time.* They all line up at the front entrance of the housing area to receive their prescribed meds for the day and then, bam! It's like the house has done a 360-degree turn. No more yelling at the television or nothing, just the walking dead.

Then an inmate sitting nearby starts to talk to me about his case as if I'm interested. I entertain him because, hell, what else do I have to do. He tells me that he shot eight people in the Fort Greene projects because they raped his daughter. I take a look at him and all I see is an old man with salt-and-pepper hair and glasses that are held together by tape. My assessment, no killer here, but then again, what does a killer look like? He sees the look of disbelief on my face and decides to show me proof. So off he goes to his cell to retrieve what inmates call "paperwork." These are the court papers that officially tell why an inmate is incarcerated. They are so official that if they ain't right, meaning if an inmate has paperwork that names him as a snitch, it could mean death. As he runs off I'm thinking, *Great, besides being a babysitter, a judge, and a counselor, now I am a fucking psychiatrist.* We wear many hats doing this job. While he's at his cell, I take this time to go to the back of the housing area so that I can get a signal on my cell phone and check my messages.

BEEP, the first one is from Bryant. The murder, from what I hear, is still being investigated, and she sounds hysterical: *Yo, these fools are really trying some bullshit! I learn that King is covering Fran by saying that he was on the A side of the housing area when the inmate got killed on the B side. This takes Fran out of the equation as to whose fault this was and still leaves me out there! They both know that when I rolled up into the area both of them was in the officers' station and what's bugging me out is why neither one of them is stepping up and saying that I had nothing to do with this shit. And guess what, they suspended me indefinitely! Yo, hit me when you get off.*

BEEP, second message is from Mom Dukes: *I smelled you when you used the bathroom before you left this morning. You need to drink some water, boy!*

BEEP, there are no more messages. I shake my head. Where would I be without messages like that?

I go back to the dayroom feeling sorry for Bryant, because it's bullshit like this that makes a person hate this job. I mean, for me, the job is mad easy. Shoot, coming from where I come from, it's just like hanging on the block. But now, I'm looking at what they're trying to do to Bryant and the job just doesn't seem so prestigious. I'm hustling, Rains is selling ass, and Bryant is getting framed. There's a lot going on, to say the least.

I observe a young inmate as he stands up, goes over to the corner of the room with his drinking cup, and then seems to take a piss in it. I jump up and yell, "What the fuck are you doing?" My shouting brings the female A officer running onto the floor. Then the inmate does the unthinkable. Right there while we are all watching, he drinks his piss. My face cringes at the act, imagining what that must taste like. The A officer just sucks her teeth and says, "Again, Davis?" Then she storms off to the officers' station and gets on the phone. I'm stunned, standing there like a chick looking at a horror flick alone late at night. The inmate looks at me and finishes his drink like it's the last call for alcohol at the bar. The A officer comes back inside and tells the inmate to lock in. He obeys and goes to his cell.

The A officer turns to look at me and laughs when she sees the look on my face. She explains to me that these inmates pull stunts like that all the time. She says that a lot of them, like inmate Davis, who's facing a lot of time, do these things to try to convince a judge that they're crazy and can't be tried like sane people.

"Hey, sometimes it works and sometimes it don't," she explains.

She goes down to the inmate's cell and yells, "They're not coming!" On her way back to the officers' station she tells me that he did that in front of me so that I would have to write a report that I witnessed him doing that to himself. She said that he could use that report to help his insanity case, but that the doctors were not coming to get him to evaluate him because they have already deemed him fit to stand trial for two murders he committed on the Lower East Side.

"Now this fool is banging his head against the cell door to get attention," she says.

I shake my head and go sit down. Some of the less sedated inmates are still trying to figure out which of the well-dressed men are really women and which ones they would fuck. That's when the killer that looks like "Pop from the corner store" comes back with his paperwork. I sigh and take a look at it, because I know that he won't leave me alone if I don't. The papers are stapled together neatly and in order, and as I go through them I see drawings of the bodies he shot as they lay out all through the apartment.

He's sitting next to me narrating each and every picture, telling me who died and how he caught this one or that one off guard. A chill is running through me, thinking about how calm he is when he talks about it. The stench rises in my nose like one of these derelicts just farted but I don't look up because one of them is always letting loose. Hey, that's jail for you. I try to continue to read, but the smell is just too strong, so I finally look up to see if I can identify where the smell is coming from and *Bam!* The sight right there next to me turns my stomach, and my lunch begins to come up out of my mouth and nose. The inmate that was telling me about his paperwork was sitting there with shit smeared all over his face and clothes. I jump up and continue to let my guts spill out all over the floor. He gets up and grabs his papers so that I won't mess them up and sits back down and continues to narrate his story without a care in the world, and I can see that he has chunks of shit still in his mouth.

The A officer again comes inside and sees this, then runs back to the station and gets on the phone. I run into the officers' bathroom. While I wash up, I vow to never work this area again. *Fuck the overtime! This is blood money!* I come out of the bathroom just in time to see him being escorted out in a straitjacket. The officer asks me if I am alright and I nod yes, but I'm really not.

I go back to sit down and pray that this tour ends soon. After a while when all the excitement dies down I decide to make a tour of the area and check inside each cell to make sure that the inmates that are locked in are okay. I routinely flash my light in each cell to see inside and right now most of the inmates that are in their cells are curled up sleeping off their medication.

As I come to one particular cell, I notice the light is out and the inmate is sitting on the floor with his back against the wall right under his window. I don't pay it any mind at first because I'm used to just walking by and peeking in the cells. Then I remember that this is the inmate that earlier was banging his head against the door of his cell to get attention. I think I'd better go double-check. So I double back to his cell and flash my light inside. He is still on the floor, sitting there with his head hanging down. Then I notice the thin string that comes up behind his head and connects to the window knob. I yell for the A officer to crack his cell open and hit the lights. When she does, I rush in and see that his face is turning purple. He was trying to hang himself by sitting down and leaning his head forward so that the string would draw tight around his neck. I cut the string from around his neck while yelling out what happened to the A officer.

The inmate has lost color in his face and he appears not to be breathing when I pick him up and lay him on his bed. I am panicking, because if he is dead, we are going to be in a world of shit because we are supposed to be giving these fools an option to go into their cells every hour and this allows us to check on them to prevent shit like this. Then I hear her walking, not running, down the walkway toward the cell. I hear her yelling to me before she gets there, saying, "Heyward, you're stressing these fools too much. This is probably another one of their stunts to get attention because they can't get their way." When she gets to the cell I look at her like, "Bitch, does this look like a stunt to you?" Her eyes light up and she runs off to go call the clinic. I stand over him, panicking, saying to myself, "Let me think! Let me think!"

Then I think to myself that I have to try that rescue breathing shit that I was taught, not in the Academy but as a marine. So I proceed to follow the steps. I kneel down and put my finger to his nose to see if he is breathing. He isn't. *No, that's wrong. You're supposed to look and see if his chest rises and falls.* So I step back so I can look at his chest. Shit, I really can't tell. So I just assume that he isn't breathing and start CPR.

I don't really remember any of this shit! Is it five breaths and fifteen pumps on the chest or is the count one one thousand, two one thousand? Shit, how am I supposed to hold my hands? Where am I supposed to put them, and am I doing this shit right? I start to pump right below his chest but not on top of his stomach. I get no response.

This shit seems like an eternity but all this is happening in seconds. I brace myself, because I know that I have to do some nasty shit right now that I know that I don't want to do and that instrument in the officers' station that I could use has not been changed in years and it looks dirtier than this inmate's mouth. I have to give him some air. I get up and, with my hands on my hips, look off into space and try to psych myself up to do this. I look at his chest again, praying that I see it rise and fall. I say out loud as I am looking, "God, please give me something." Then I peek outside the cell. *Where is the clinic staff?*

Come on, stupid ass, you can do this! I kneel down to him, clamp his nose, tilt his head back, and give him a breath, look away, then give him another. I feel like I'm not doing the shit right. I step back to see if he's breathing now. No bueno!

I'm about to do it again when he takes a deep breath and coughs. I'm stunned and don't know what to do, so I stand there with my fist clinched and wait. He begins to cough some more. His eyes open and close and then he starts to breathe normally. I jump up and down and pump my fist. He opens his eyes and looks around like, "Where am I?" and without hesitation kicks off his shoes, pulls his covers over himself, and gets comfortable to go to sleep.

The medical staff finally comes to get him. He's looking at them crazy as they put him on a gurney and roll him out. Mind you, he has the mark around his neck from the string. I go sit in the officers' station and tell the A officer what I had just done and guess what, she doesn't believe that I put my lips on this dirty inmate's mouth. At this point I don't give a shit, because I'd rather fill out paperwork for an attempted suicide than an actual one.

Shortly after, our area captain arrives and we fill her in on what just happened. She, too, breathes a sigh of relief and tells me to walk with her while she makes a tour of the area. We get to the dayroom and she starts barking at the inmates, giving them orders to do this and do that, and to clean this up and clean that up, and she scolds me for not having them do so myself. When she's about to leave, an elderly inmate, known for not talking to anyone, calls out my name. We both turn around, stunned, to see what he has to say. Pointing to the captain, he stutters, "Tha, that thatbitchisaman!"

BY ANY MEANS NECESSARY

Two months later . . .

It's a Wednesday, so I know the visiting floor will be popping. I'm on my way to my post from roll call and as usual I'm dirty with pouches stuffed in my vest.

"Put ya hands on that fuckin' wall," an officer yells at an inmate.

Whatever is happening with the officer and that inmate is the last thing I want to deal with right now. Technically, an officer in this situation should stop and stand there as a show of force to the inmate, because if he acts up he can and will catch a beatdown. But I got a big load on me and I really need to get to my post to set up shop.

I stand there and watch the officer go off on the inmate. He calls him a lowlife because he's in jail. He tells him how much better he is than him because he's an officer, how much money he's making, and so on. I typically wouldn't have a problem with what the officer is saying about the money he's making, but I know this officer. He gets his drink on like me. He's married and living with his wife's family until they can get their own apartment. At his wedding reception they served us ketchup and syrup sandwiches. So, he wasn't exactly ballin'.

I really don't have time for this shit, so I ask him what we are doing. In other words, are we taking him down or what? The officer turns to me and says, "Nah, I just wanted to show him that he can get it at any . . ."

Before he can finish his sentence, I'm on my way to my post—and I'm not looking back. I get to my post, take my count, and relieve the midnight officer so that I can take care of business. Things had changed. Gone was the scared-for-his-job officer that would never do anything to violate his sacred job. Gone was the officer that was nervous every time he walked through those gates carrying contraband. And gone was the man that stood idly by and did nothing as child support sucked him dry and ruined his life. In his place was a man that was no longer on defense but on offense; a man that now ran an organization composed of trustworthy inmates and one female officer; a man that was no longer fueled by need but by greed.

I had gotten so used to making money every day that even when the child support leveled out and I could've probably survived off just what I was making from the pouches, I couldn't stop. My lifestyle had changed, too. I had my own apartment now. I had bought a late-model used car that didn't look half bad and I had the shakes (gambling problem) like never before, so stopping wasn't an option. Plus, now I enjoyed it. I lived to come to work and collect and run my day-to-day enterprise.

I let Flocko and Moe out. I make the drop along with two bacon, egg, and cheese sandwiches. I learned from the streets that you have to take care of your workers and they will take care of you. As Flocko walks away with the pouches, I hear a door swing open and somebody scream out, "Search!"

Shit!

It was one of those surprise searches. They came through the fire door and not the front gate entrance to my housing area. Damn, they already had all the inmates coming out of their cells, lined up with their hands on the wall. Now I'm standing inside the officers' station watching them go one by one searching the inmates and their cells. I can see Flocko from where I'm standing, peeking down the hall at me. He has a lot of pouches on him and I know that if he gets caught right now I will be questioned or looked at suspiciously.

I have to do something.

I'm pacing back and forth. I see that they are getting close to searching Flocko when I get an idea and spring into action. It's risky but I have to try something. I go onto the floor where they're searching and walk toward him and when I get there I start to curse him out, saying, "I got this one, because he likes to run his mouth." I aggressively pat him down. I yell at him and say, "If you open your mouth I'm a bust yo ass!" As always I play it right, because I could see the other officers that were from other jails looking at me and praying that I wouldn't start shit with this inmate. I know that they know better than to get into a use of force in a jail other than their own.

Officers were always told not to start shit outside their jail, because when it comes down to writing reports and coming up with lies to cover your ass, you'd rather they come from officers from your jail that you have a bond with, that you trust.

I order Flocko to stand across the hall as he witnesses me searching his cell. The captain and the other officers just assume that Flocko is an asshole and that I am taking advantage of the situation to get back at an unruly inmate while I had major backup. After I half-ass mess up his cell, I order him to go sit on his bed and I lock his cell behind him just as the other officers were doing with the other inmates.

Mission accomplished.

The facial expression on the other inmates who were a part of my team was a look of I-can't-believe-this-nigga-just-took-that-risk-and-saved-Flocko's-ass. It was also a look of loyalty, that Big Hey was real about his business. I breathe easier once the search is over and the visiting officers leave. I'm glad everything is over and we didn't get busted, because I need my money. After the inmates clean up the housing postsearch, I go to Flocko's cell to see why the money has been coming up short as of late.

As I'm walking, I peek into some other cells. I notice Aak on his knees praying and in the next cell is Murder putting up his towel preparing for a massive beatdown upon his penis. I continue to walk and I see two relatively young inmates standing in the corridor with no shirts on listening to the radio. They're sharing a clear plastic radio that is sold at commissary and both are deep into reciting the words to the song, yelling out, "I ain't no killa but don't push me/revenge is like the sweetest joy next to getting pussy." I give them the hand gesture like, "Keep it down" and they nod in the affirmative.

I approach Flocko's cell. I hear voices coming out of it indicating that there is more than one inmate in his cell. I'm thinking they are probably having a smoke session.

As I get closer to his door, though, I hear a scuffle inside and then I hear Flocko say, "Give it up!" I peek in to see what's going on. I am shocked at what I see. Flocko and two other inmates have an inmate bent over the bed with the inmate's pants pulled down. Two of them pin the inmate down while Flocko is on his knees. Flocko is fully clothed and is off to the side of the pinned inmate. By now I'd been working here for a while and I'd caught inmates before in several disgusting sex acts, so that was no surprise. But I never figured Flocko to be that type. I'd look farther in and it appears that Flocko has his fingers going inside this inmate's ass. I bang on the door and they all jump. The two inmates who are holding the inmate down release him, but Flocko does not let go until he pulls something out of the inmate's butt. I open the door and they stand there, unsure of what is going to happen next. I'm heated. The only person I want to talk to is Flocko.

I yell, "Everybody out!"

One by one, they all file out. When the assaulted inmate walks past I can see the shame and embarrassment on his face. I ask him if he needs medical attention. He shakes his head, indicating no, as Flocko says, "Hey, he knows what it is; that it wasn't personal, but all business."

"Business?" I ask.

"Yeah, Hey, this is jail, and if you want to survive you got to always know what's poppin' and be able to do what you got to do to survive," Flocko said.

I look at him like he's crazy and say, "Flock, I understand all that and I know that you have been in here awhile. It's just that I never thought . . ." He sees where I'm going with this and cuts me off by bursting out laughing. He says, "Gee, this is me, Gee! You think I am in here fuckin' niggas!?" Again he laughs and says, "No, Gee, seriously though, my man saw him boofing this on the visit." He raises his hand, showing me a ball of something wrapped in plastic with a little shit on it. His facial expression has no shame or remorse about the fact that he has another man's shit on his fingers.

Mental note: From now on, Flocko will definitely get the closed-fist bump when we greet, no more soul brother number five and shakes at all.

"Don't nothing come through 8 upper without me knowing about it or getting my cut," he says.

Then he points to the inmate that just had his colon checked and says, "That fool knows that! He's just a fucking mule. His asshole is the size of Kansas. That's what he does. That's his job."

Since he is acting like the boss of all bosses, I take this time to ask him why was the money, which I am supposed to be getting, coming up short all of a sudden.

"I was going to talk to you about that," he says. "This is what that's about."

Then he holds up the bundle and opens the shitty package so I can see what is on the inside. Cocaine. With his hands in the air as if I was sticking him up, he says to me, "First, I just want you to know that somebody on the dorm side is cutting your throat."

"What do you mean, another inmate?" I ask, with one of my eyebrows raised, letting him know that I am getting pissed.

"Yep," he says. "And he got better prices. Every inmate that's over on that side is rocking with him now. So that is why our flow done slowed up. And if he's getting it like I am getting it, ya know what that means, right?"

I am in deep thought when he says that, because I know exactly what he means. It was stupid of me to think that I would be the only one rocking like this. While holding up the coke he continues and says, "This is what's popping right now, Gee. This is where the money is at and everybody and their momma is getting that paper up to get it." He stood there looking at me, knowing that I know what he is getting at.

"That's a whole new ball game," I say, staring at him.

"I'm ready if you're ready," Flocko says.

I tell him that I will think about it. As I'm walking away, he says, "Scared money don't make no money."

CHAPTER 34

MY BROTHER'S KEEPER

BUMP, BUMP, BUMP, BUMP!

I can hear my heart beating loud and clear. I'm outside by the bowling alley close to Rikers Island about to meet Flocko's sister. I'm a little nervous because this is my first trip picking up coke. Cigarettes and pouches of tobacco were different, because if I get stopped in the street with those I won't get charged, but if I get stopped with a half ounce of cocaine, I'm screwed. I'm sitting there sipping when my phone rings. It's her telling me that she's pulling up. I haven't seen her in years and really forgot what she looked like.

I exit my van when I see a woman park and begin to walk toward me. She stops a few cars from mine. I walk up to her.

"Hey, what's up? Long time no see," she says.

I still don't recognize her, but looking at her face I can see the likeness between her and Flocko.

"That's a half," she says. I just nod in acknowledgment, taking the bag from her.

"Okay. I got it," I tell her.

Then she walks back to her car and I get into mine and just like that I become a drug dealer.

After the transaction I drive home in silence. Just me and my thoughts. I just made fifteen hundred dollars in less than fifteen minutes and it feels great. After a while my adrenaline finally slows down. I start calculating my future earnings; one trip a week with this and I'm good.

I get to my neighborhood and as usual there is no parking. I find the nearest fire hydrant and park right in front of it, putting my Rikers Island parking pass in the window. I proceed toward my building, but I'm cautious, because it hasn't been normal since the attempt on my life. It's been real stressful coming and going, always think-ing that this fool Biz is lurking somewhere in the cut. This shit with Biz had me frustrated and angry. I didn't like having to be on point like that all the time; holstering my weapon, putting it in my jacket pocket so if it came down to him or me, it was most definitely going to be him.

I'd started taking different routes from the parking lot to my building so that I couldn't be tracked. I would never come home at the same time. I would use different entrances to get inside the building. And I would do things like press the elevator button of the floor above or below mine so that I could come out somewhere other than my floor.

I cautiously enter my building and, surprisingly, an elevator is on the ground floor waiting. I run and jump inside just as the door closes behind me. I press the button for two floors beneath mine, because I know that the staircase door on that floor doesn't make a sound when you open it. When the elevator arrives at the floor, I press the door-open button and stand there inside the elevator with-out moving. I purposely wait for the door to close, and when it does I jump out. This maneuver would throw off and surprise anyone who might be waiting there for me. I was taught these maneuvers from one of my gambling spot siblings that had beef in every project. I remember him saying, "Whatever you do, don't make it easy for them, Gee." And I wasn't.

I make my way down the hallway to the silent door and exit. It's a good thing I had on my uniform with my windbreaker jacket and my work boots, which were more like sneakers. They didn't protect my feet from shit but they didn't make a lot of noise either. Inside the stairwell I hear someone talking on the floors above me.

I take my gun out of my pocket, put it to my side, and begin to creep up the stairs. Two steps at a time because I want to move swiftly. I'm close when I realize it's just one voice. Whoever it is isn't talking but singing. It's "Am I My Brother's Keeper." A song I used to sing as a kid.

Biz!

Now my adrenaline is flowing. My heart starts pounding and my palms get sweaty. This is it. I get closer. Step by step, all I can think about is him trying to kill me and me being stressed out trying to duck this fool all the time. All the stealth training I received from the marines comes into play, because I am going to put an end to this shit right here, right now. My conscience starts to talk to me: *Gee, are you really going to do this? Is this what it has come to?* I creep. His singing gets louder, "Am I my brother's keeper!" I think some more and question myself. *What are you going to do? Are you going to shoot him? Are you built like this?* Everybody in every hood knows that old saying: "Don't pull a gun out unless you plan to use it." *Should I do this?* After all this time I have the drop on this fool and it's late night in the hood and that makes for a perfect opportunity.

I stop. I can still hear him singing. He's right above me. I have my gun raised, but now I bring it down to my side. The stairs are built with a landing between floors and I'm standing there silently with my gun and my target right above me. Anger and urgency come over me. I remember the ultimate no-no that this fool committed. He threatened my family, most of all, my momma in that elevator. I'm nervous. I am scared, and right now my stomach is filled with rocks.

Yes, I am built like this!

I raise my gun and lean to the side so I can peer up the steps. He's sitting there with his back to me singing and doing something with his hands that I cannot see. I got him. I can blast his ass right now, right in the back, and get away with it. No, I want this fool to see me. I want him to know that I did this to him.

I take a step closer, then out of nowhere he says, "Remember that song, Gee? We used to sing it all the time."

CHAPTER 35

HEARTFELT

It seemed like an eternity had gone by as I stood there, gun in hand, dumbfounded that he knew I was there the whole time. No need for stealth now. I climbed up the rest of the steps, positioning myself directly in front of him. I still had my gun pointed at him when I noticed what he was doing. There was a cardboard box laid across his lap with a blunt cut opened and filled with weed. He took a vial of crack from his pocket and sprinkled it into the blunt—mind you, never once looking up at me to see that I had my gun pointed at him. I felt that he already knew. He began to hum that song again as he brought the woolly to his mouth. He wet it so that it rolled tight. Then, and only then, did he look up at me to see my menacing stare.

"You ain't never been no killa, Gee. And you sure don't look like one now," he said, laughing.

"What does a killa look like, Biz?" I asked with venom in my voice.

He put his blunt in his mouth, lit it, and blew out smoke while nodding at me like he got my point.

"Now what?" he asked. "Ya got ya little peashooter pointed at me like ya ready to end me. Now what?"

He threw his arms in the air. I jumped back at the sight of a sawed-off shotgun. I had not seen it under the cardboard. He laughed again as he put his arms down and took some more puffs. While exhaling, he said, "Don't be scared now. Ya should have been scared the other night when you came out of the gambling spot at two in the morning or the other night when you parked on 153rd Street and walked to the back of the building entrance." He saw the dumbfounded look on my face and said, "I could have gotten you anytime I wanted to."

I put my gun down—not away, just down. Truthfully, he and I both knew that I wasn't going to do shit. He took the blunt out of his mouth and pointed it at me.

"Why you do that shit to me, Gee? I mean, I've been jailing my whole life and I know how dirty COs can be but I never thought that you would do me dirty like that."

"I did not know it was you under that same dirty hoodie that you're wearing now," I tried to explain. "How was I supposed to know that they transferred you to my jail, huh?"

He jumped up and said, "You know how it felt seeing that it was you who did this to me?" He pulled his hood off, showing his permanent scars.

"And then you just stood there!" he shouted. "Stood there and did nothing! You did nothing while those white boys pounded on me. Was that that blue brotherhood bullshit? You beat on me to prove to the white man that you had no problem beating on a nigga?"

I saw the pain in his face and I decided not to respond. "What was you afraid of, huh?" He answered his own question and said, "You were afraid that if you stepped in to stop them that you would not be respected as one of them!" Now he was sweating and he had his hood halfway off his face, staring up into the light fixture. My assumption was that the drug was kicking in and he was high. I put my gun away and leaned back against the wall. I began to question whether he was right about some of the things he was saying.

"Were your CO buddies there, Gee?" he asked. "Were they there when we had to share clothes? When I would come to your house and you come to mine when our families did not have food? Were they there when we got jumped by some guys trying to take your sneakers? Who took that ass-whipping with you? Who?"

Now we were both staring hard at one another, both of us knowing the answer.

"You think this shit is easy?" I yelled. "You think it's easy seeing your friends and loved ones come to jail? Seeing them go back and forth all the time not learning their lesson the first time and constantly fucking up in life? Just imagine busting your ass trying to stay out of trouble in the neighborhood and area that we came up in; landing this job and then seeing your people get their ass beat not by you but by other people." I laid into him. "Look at you, Biz. You want to blame everyone but yourself for you coming back and forth to jail. Do you ever think of the shit that you do while you're out? Do you think of the people that you hurt when you get locked up? Huh!? You know what your moms once told me?"

He froze, looked at me hard, and began tearing up at the mention of his mother. I had found a soft spot and now I was going to twist my knife. I continued, "She told me one day that if I saw you in there for me to tell you that she loves you and that she is getting old and that she don't know how much longer she can take you being in there." Now he had his head down and he began to sway from side to side. Then I said in a low, heartfelt voice, "It was a mistake, man.

I did not know that it was you until your hoodie came off." Then he said, without looking up at me, "A mistake, huh? So what would you have done had you known it was me before they started whipping my ass?"

Dead silence. I had no response. Then he said, "Them mutha-fuckas are going to pay. Them COs think that they can do anything to a person while they are in prison and that a person won't come after their asses when they get out. They think moving up to Middle-town or out to Long Island will stop an inmate from finding them. Humph, I got something for their asses. They're going to pay for what they did to me." I then ask him, "What are you going to do, sue them?" He responded by handing me a piece of paper out of his pocket, and when I looked it had a list of COs' names with their addresses next to them. My first thought was *Oh, shit, how did he get this info!* Then I thought, *I can't let this happen.* I began to yell at him frantically, "See, this is what I am talking about! You still on some bullshit that's going to have your ass back in jail or worse."

He wasn't paying me any mind. He was gathering his things and taking long pulls from his blunt. Meanwhile, I continued to yell, "Why can't you just let this shit go and get your shit together?"

He just smiled at me, picked up his sawed-off shotgun, and put it over his shoulder as if it was a mere handbag. He took off down the steps. Halfway down, with his back toward me, he said, "I love you, Gee." I just continued to yell at his back, "What about your moms? Don't you think that she's had enough? You're going to put her through this shit again?" He stopped in his tracks, turned around, and looked up at me. He was crying. I saw the tears running down his face. He pulled his hoodie all the way over his head and said, "She won't be going through any more pain because of me."

"Why you say that?" I asked. "Do you think this time will be any easier?"

"She died this morning," he said without looking up at me.

Then he walked down the stairs, exited onto one of the floors, and was gone.

CHAPTER 36

NO-JOKE

The next morning I arrived at work carrying my first shipment of coke. As usual, in the morning there was a line to check weapons before we went through the metal detector. As I stood there awaiting my turn, I noticed a white officer, who graduated with me, casually standing on the other side of the metal detector. Something was not right. As I recalled, though he graduated with me, as soon as we were assigned to our respective jails, he disappeared, nowhere to be found. Then, oh, shit, it came to me. He went straight to the K-9 Unit to train drug-sniffing dogs, and if I was a betting man, I'd bet he had his sniffer right there, under the desk by the entrance, out of sight so no one could see it. Damn, what was I going to do now with a half ounce of coke on me? I had to think fast. Luckily for me there were some lockers by the front door for visiting lawyers to put away their cell phones and other stuff prohibited inside the jail. I moved quickly while the hustle and bustle of officers going through the detector was happening. I hurried and put a brown paper bag filled with coke in one of the lockers. I returned to the line, turned in my firearm, and proceeded through the detector. The detector beeped because I'm in full uniform—shield and all. I passed through and said what's up to the officer that I knew. I looked down to see old

Smokey, a large German shepherd, just lying under the desk, in the cut, with his tongue hanging out, just waiting to catch someone. I breezed through and went to the locker room to wait until he and his dog left.

I got to the locker room, where a group of officers were having another Norman-Seabrook-is-useless ceremony while everyone was getting dressed. (Norman Seabrook was then president of the Correction Officers' Benevolent Association.) I don't understand why they even bother, as everyone who opposes him loses, and none of the allegations against him were ever proven. But, hey, if they want to sit there and whoop and holler, so be it.

I was going through the motions at this point, waiting for roll call to start so that I could retrieve my package. Afterward I walked back out, got the coke, and walked back in. Rin Tin Tin, the K-9 dog, was gone. The whole time the front entrance officer only glanced up from reading the paper long enough to see that it was someone in uniform going back and forth. I made it to my post and made the drop to Flocko. He assured me that as soon as movement was allowed this morning it would be out of my housing area.

So I sat back on my post in the A station, breathing a little easier. I had some time to relax a minute before I let the inmates out. I began to think about my mother and how hard she took it when I told her last night about Ms. Daniels's death. I just shook my head at the fact that my own mother was getting up there in age and that another one of her friends had passed away. Then I thought about Biz's CO hit list. I debated whether I should take his threat seriously. What were the chances of his being able to carry out the hits? Did he just smoke crack in front of me so I would think he was on some high shit, not being serious? But he did have a list of addresses that would make one wonder how he got it.

I had let the inmates out to start my day. One by one I clicked open the cells and received the normal rush of inmates, all wanting something at the same time.

CO, open the shower!

CO, I need this. CO, I need that!

It becomes like Grand Central Station in a matter of minutes. After I wrote out the passes, Flocko came up to the officers' station to tell me that the bird had flown the coop. The coke was out of the housing area via his personal mule. He said that he needed to holla at me. So we went into our office where we conduct business, which is him inside the utility closet, and me pretending that I'm telling him what to do in there. He told me how much I could get by letting inmates use my phone to make calls that they can't make on the city inmate monitored phones. I told him that I would think about it. I already knew off the bat that they weren't using my phone, but maybe I could find a phone that would work.

"On the gate," I heard an officer yell. I turned to see that I was receiving a new inmate into my housing area. I cracked the gate open and they both walked in.

The officer gave me the inmate's locator card, and because we didn't know each other, there was no conversation, just a nod, and then he left. The inmate was a young slim dude with braids. He was ice grilling me. I could already see that he was going to be a problem. I paid it no mind, because a lot of times the ice grill is just a front to intimidate other inmates. I did the usual orientation, then I told him what cell to go to. I buzzed him in and he went to his cell. Then he stepped right back out with his shirt off. He started asking who ran the phones and about slot time. I told him I ran the phones and he grilled me through the protective gate and started going off, disrespecting me, talking about how he didn't trust Po-Po and how his fellow inmates shouldn't either, how every chance that he gets he tries to put a shank in a CO's neck.

I stood there and watched him talk. Then Flocko came up to the front and we made eye contact. I shook my head, laughing, as the inmate continued mouthing off, trying to recruit other inmates to join his act. None of them budged. In fact, I could see Flocko sending out orders with just his eye movement.

My B officer went to the other side of the housing area to give them an option of letting the inmates go to their cells to retrieve stuff. Now the inmate was openly challenging me, saying that he was about to turn it up and make it hot in here. I sat back in my seat and just watched him run his mouth. Then Flocko asked if he could talk to him. I figured Flocko was going to calm him down, let him know how things were run around here. Flocko put his arm around the inmate's shoulders and told him to chill out. Then one of Flocko's soldiers came up and handed the guy a girlie magazine. In my mind there is nothing that calms a situation down better than cooch. Flocko had his arm around the inmate's shoulders, talking to him while he pointed out something in the magazine. I looked down at my logbook for a split second. When I looked up I saw Flocko spit something out of his mouth, across the inmate's face, into his own hand, and then jerk his hand back real fast.

The move was so smooth and swift that if you blinked you would've missed it. I heard the inmate yelp, then saw him grab his face. It was already too late, because the blood was already squirting out and I could see the slit opening wider as he grabbed his jaw and began to yell uncontrollably. I jumped up in shock and yelled for everyone to lock in. I saw Flocko and his goons do as I said real quick. I called for the B officer to lock in the side that he was on as well, then come over to my side.

I immediately pressed my body alarm and called the clinic for medical attention. I rushed onto the floor, where the inmate was now squirming around, holding the flesh that was hanging off his face. The captain and the medical team arrived at the same time, along with several officers who I knew were going to perform an immediate search of the area. The captain ordered me to accompany the inmate to the clinic along with the staff to ensure that he would not act up along the way. It was a short trip to the clinic and the inmate lay still the whole way, quietly staring up at the ceiling, with makeshift bloody bandages wrapped around his head holding his jaw together.

At the clinic the medics rushed the inmate to the back, where they began to work on him. I was told by the clinic officer that my captain called and said that he would be needing a report on the incident. I knew it was coming. It would be real simple, all the B officer had to say was that he was on the other side and did not see anything. All I had to say was that it happened in the back of the housing area, so I did not see who did it either. The fact was that there were only two officers watching sixty to a hundred inmates at any given time. So there is no way humanly possible for an officer to see everything that goes on. This is why it's always easy for an officer not to assume any liability for what happens to an inmate.

The captain arrived at the clinic just as a nurse came running to the front frantically asking for assistance restraining the inmate. I followed the captain into the room in the back, where we found the inmate sitting up on the edge of the table. The nurse was trying to apply some more gauze to his face to control the bleeding until they could get him to a hospital to get stitched up. The more she tried, the more he moved his face, not wanting her to touch him. The captain then said, "Nojockal Turner," calling him by his government name, "who did this to you?" The inmate looked at me, the captain, and the nurse real hard before he tore off the gauze and exposed his wound. We all jumped back, because blood began to come out as he ran his tongue back and forth into the cut, which was so big now that we could see his teeth and gums through it.

"My name is No-Joke," he said. "I ain't no snitch and those muthafuckas should have killed me."

CHAPTER 37

ONLY FIFTY DOLLARS

Work had become routine and for the most part I was acting like any other officer. Every now and then I would attend a CO function or attempt to play on the jail's basketball team. I was blending in and no one was suspecting me of doing anything outside my everyday duties. The conditions were ripe for hustling to become a primary source of income. There was plenty of time and space. I had one foot in the jail as a CO, another in the streets between my hustles and the gambling spot.

I was now bringing in either coke or tobacco whenever I worked. They were mandatory. The coke game, particularly, was really paying off. I was making a substantial amount of money on a daily basis, which supplemented my corrections officer paycheck.

I also found ways to further increase my revenue. Rarely did an inmate have that ride-or-die chick who would take the risk of bringing him contraband, so the inmate would have his peeps Western Union the money to a third party whom I knew, and once I got the okay that the money was there, I would deliver the item. If it wasn't a wire transaction, I would meet the customer somewhere and he would pay me right then and there to deliver product inside for him. I was making money, but for some of these inmates, the money they made from the stuff I was bringing in was enough to support their families.

My smaller hustles were not every day though, like cell phone service for the inmates. I brought the smallest compact prepaid cell phone that I could buy and would bring it in just as I would my own cell phone. Then after receiving five hundred dollars from the inmate I would lock him in his cell and let him rock out until the minutes ran out. I didn't care who they called, because most of the time it was either their lawyer or some girl to discuss things that they could not say over the inmate monitored phones.

Things ran smooth, too. I even had the mess hall workers come pick up in the morning so that they could make sales at the lunch-time feeding. I had the inmates that went to either recreation or the law library making transactions for me throughout the jail. Occasionally I had to issue an ass-whipping to a nondescript (an inmate with no affiliation, or one who had no influence) who I thought was too nosy or who might jeopardize my operation. If my employees performed well I would reward them with something like a drink of liquor or maybe some food from outside. And from time to time I'd still hear about what other COs were doing, but it did not matter because my organization was a close-knit one, and ran like clockwork.

Since my housing area was a high-classification area, I had no problem finding loyal street gang members to hustle with. Most of their charges were attempted murder, murder, or some form of drug kingpin charge. No slouches here. I treated them fairly and with respect, because no matter what crime they committed, I still considered them men. Plus, they were already incarcerated and going through trial and they might never see the light of day again, so there was no need for me to stress them over petty jail shit. I began doing business with them mainly because Flocko had gotten sentenced to a ten-to-twenty for his attempted-murder charge and was waiting to go up north.

One day I'd gotten off work and was on my way to Queens to collect five hundred dollars from an inmate's grandmother. It was his birthday and he wanted a half pint of liquor and some red velvet cake. I followed her directions and pulled up over by the 40 Projects. I spotted her standing on the corner in front of a grocery store in the clothes that she said that she'd be wearing. I pulled up in my van and rolled down the window. She came up to my van and said, "Gee?" I responded with a nod. She smiled and got in. I checked her out for a moment. She had salt-and-pepper hair. Her age showed on her face, but she still looked good for a woman who I guessed was in her fifties. She had on a short jacket and jeans that displayed the fact that she kept in shape, or at least it appeared that way. She started talking to me, asking about her grandson, if he was okay and where he was, and were we treating him right, and so on. I answered with, "I wouldn't be here if he wasn't being treated right." She smiled and began to thank me as we pulled away from the curb to go somewhere secluded to finish our transaction. She started talking to me about her grandson going in and out of jail and reassuring me that I'm safe with her because this is not the first time she has met up with a CO or used Western Union to pay for something to help her grandson. She told me that the way she looked at it, I'm down for the people. She said only real COs never forget where they come from and recognize how hard it is to maintain out here. She went on to say that I provided a service that allowed families who can't afford to take care of their loved ones with commissary money every two weeks to do something to help them. I acknowledged that when someone paid me a hundred dollars for two or three pouches of tobacco, their loved one could juggle them and trade them for commissary, that the money could last him for months, thus taking some of the burden off the family.

I parked a few blocks down from where I picked her up so that I could get this over with and be on my way. She handed me the liquor and the cake and before she handed me the money she said, "Um, the money is a little short." I gave her a look like, "I don't want to hear that shit." Then I asked, with one eyebrow up, "How short?" She said, "Only fifty dollars. It's because they cut my food stamps this week and I did not have that many of them to sell to get all the money up." I counted the money. It was $450. I was about to tell her it was cool when she leaned over into my ear and said, "There's other ways to get paid, baby." Then she licked my ear.

I looked at her like, "You're this dude's grandmother, and what I look like doing something like that?" She sat back in her seat and said, "I'll do anything to make sure my baby is alright." Then she put her thumb in her mouth. I'm stuck, just sitting there with the money, the liquor, and the cake in my hands. She looked around to see who was around then leaned over into my lap and started to unbuckle my belt. Guess what? I did not stop her.

I leaned my seat back and closed my eyes, thinking, *Damn, I made some good money in the jail today and this is an extra couple of dollars to throw in with it* (not to mention that she was serious with what she was doing). It felt eerie seeing her salt-and-pepper hair go up and down. Eerie and good, real good, so good that it took me two seconds to upchuck and release my tadpoles. When it was over she raised up and just smiled, didn't say a word while I drove back to where I picked her up. I pulled over, she got out and waved. I sat there for a minute putting the stuff away, and then she came back and knocked on the window. I gave her a confused look as I rolled down the window. Then she pointed to my dashboard and my eyes widened when I saw why her performance was so good. Sitting up there near my window was a full set of dentures! She had gummed me. She reached in and grabbed them, then smiled wide, showing no teeth. I shook my head and pulled off, thinking about my day.

Later that day, my money is right and I have that itch to shake them up! Dice, that is. First, I have to apply rule number one: Never go into the gambling spot with all your money. This way, if you lose, you still have something stashed. So I head home first, and I figure while I'm there I'll check up on my kids. I knock on my baby momma's door several times but there is no answer. Then while I'm standing there, the peephole cover moves to the side and then slides back. Still no one answers. I just laugh it off, because I'm done getting heated over the dumb shit, so I go around the corner to my apartment.

Once inside I take a deep whiff of whatever it is Momma is cooking. Aaaaah! I can tell that there is real fatback in them greens. I go into the living room to find my mother sitting there with this sad look on her face. I ask her what's the matter. She just starts crying. Now I am really concerned and I sit down beside her and ask her again. She says that they found a body in the back of the building today. It was Brian, known to me as Biz.

CHAPTER 38

THE PROTEST

I felt like I had just attended back-to-back funerals. First it was Biz's mother and now Biz's. I'm at work one day soon after. This particular day my mind is somewhere else thinking about everything that's happened when my phone rings. I answer it. I find out that it's my turn to press my alarm, so I get up and signal my B officer and he nods. I then press my personal protection body alarm. The inmates are unaware, because there is no alarming situation. What's happening is a demonstration organized by the officers to protest the bullshit that goes on in here with the higher-ups. It's a protest because of the unfair treatment that we have been receiving as of late, all the bogus write-ups and the tedious new rules that they were trying to implement. The sole purpose for the protest was to give the higher-ups another reason to write us up.

Yeah, it's my turn. A minute ago another housing area on the other side of the jail had pressed theirs. Every time this alarm is pulled a signal goes to the main control room to alert them that an officer is in need of help. The control room then alerts all available officers to run and assemble in the staging area with riot gear on and proceed to the problem area. Just imagine if this took place every five minutes or ten to fifteen minutes all day. I'm standing at my desk in the officers' station pretending to be doing my job when the probe team arrives at my gate. I give them a perplexed look like, "What's going on?" The captain just looks at me real serious, because he and a few out-of-breath officers already know that it's a false alarm. They're upset to be on the receiving end of this situation because false alarm or not they have to respond just in case it is not. I yell out to him, "Sorry, Cap, accidental discharge. I must have bumped it by mistake." He takes off his helmet and throws it against the wall! He's about to lay into me when a call comes in over the radio for an alarm in another housing area. He yells, "Fuck!" then scrambles to retrieve his helmet from the ground. Then he and the other officers take off in the direction of the other false alarm.

I already know that this protest isn't going to work. The only protest I heard of that did any damage was the infamous "blocking of the bridge." That was when corrections officers blocked the only bridge to Rikers Island, thus preventing anybody, including officers, from entering or leaving the Island. I wasn't there then, so I still don't know if it helped change any policies.

With the protest, the jail is on lockdown, which means there's no inmate movement. In a way, I am glad that all this is going on because I really don't feel like being there or doing shit. I had a pocket full of money when I left work that day. I was still feeling down about the death of Biz and his mother. I needed to release some stress, so I headed to the gambling spot. I was so thirsty to gamble that I went straight there, uniform still on under my windbreaker and all. I broke my number-one rule of putting some of my money up. I arrived at the spot and knocked on the door. The peephole slid to the side and I heard a voice say, "Oh, that's Gee," then I heard all kinds of locks and dead bolts being opened. It took about ten minutes for the door to open. When I went inside there was the smoke, there were the drinks, and there was the houseman yelling, "Diiiiiiicccee!" Aaaahh, music to a gambling addict's ear.

The place is packed. I go over to the gambling table and get in where I fit in. I look down at the table and see that there is a lot of money to be won. Then I say a silent prayer to the gambling gods, "Please, please let this be my night," and then I place my first bet. The guy who's holding the bank begins to shake the dice and that's when all the praying and begging of the dice begin from all the bettors. You hear, "One dice, c'mon! Ace away, dice! This nigga's arm is noodles!" All in unison. Truthfully, unless there is some crooked shit going on it's all luck. The dice get rolled and it's a head-crack. The banker wins. After the first roll this fool doesn't look back. He throws winner after winner. It takes me all of twenty minutes to lose all my money. Man, I'm so heated I'm about to black out in this funky joint. Then again the banker throws another winner. That's like six or seven in a row. I stand there thinking that something ain't right with the dice. I look at all my hard-earned money sitting over by the banker in a pile. My dumb ass risks everything to get that money, only to come in here and lose it just like that. I'm pissed at myself for hustling backward. I storm out of there with nothing more than my gun, my badge, and a wallet full of lint balls.

I go and sit in my van, which was parked right in front of the gambling spot, drinking straight from a half-gallon bottle of Hennessy and sweating like I just came out of the gym. My hand is now on my Smith and Wesson and I'm shaking my head vigorously while talking to myself. I feel cheated and I want my money back one way or another. I lean over to one side to lift up my left butt cheek so that I can let out a long-awaited fart. It seems like my stomach has cleared out some more room for me to chug-a-lug more liquid courage, and so I do. I'm numb from my pinky toe up. A Mack truck could have hit me and I wouldn't have felt it. I sit there scratching my forehead with my gun, determined and plotting to get my money back, saying to myself, "He ain't going home with what's mine." I continue to drink and watch the door, waiting for the banker to come out. Then all of a sudden I see flashing lights all around me. *Oh, shit, it's the cops.* I put my gun away and hide the open container.

My drunk ass starts to panic. Someone must have called the police, because all the cop cars come to a halt right by my van. I breathe a sigh of relief when they rush by me and run up into the gambling spot. A few moments pass as I sit there, mad as hell, as one by one the gamblers are led out, handcuffed, into the waiting police cars. My stomach sinks as I see the banker and all my money being led away to central booking. I wait until it is all clear before I take my bottle and prepare to leave. I'm about to pull off when someone knocks on my window. It's Trent, a gambling buddy of mine. I unlock my door and he gets in. We begin to finish off my bottle and talk, because he, too, had just got his money wiped out in the g-spot. We're getting sauced up when he tells me that he knows a way for us to get our money back and then some. The big-eared fucker that I am, I pay close attention to what he's saying. Any chance for me to get my paper back, I want in on it. He says he knows the banker and knows where the bank's drug spot was. He starts to formulate this plan for us to go and rob the drug spot. Mind you, Trent is not a CO, but he is a city employee just like me. I sit there still sipping and contemplating everything that he says. When he finishes laying out the plan he tells me that it's easy money.

I crank up my van and begin the drive over to the Bronx. I'm hoping I will come up with a reason, between now and the time that we reach our destination, for me to cop out and abandon the scheme. But on the real, I want my money back. I was not prepared to take a loss like I just did.

We reach the building where the drug house was located pretty quickly. We go over the game plan several times en route. Trent had been inside it before, so he knows the layout, which is how he knew it was an easy target. I park about a block away. I get out and retrieve some items that I have in the back of the van, a couple of pairs of flex cuffs, two filter masks, and a baseball cap, which I put on. I already have on my uniform and windbreaker. We walk to the building. Lucky for us, nobody is outside. We enter the building and climb some steps. When we get to the floor where the spot is located we wait for a crackhead to go cop from the spot, then we jump out on him like the police when he comes out. Mind you, we have the filter masks over our faces and my badge is hanging from my neck. I put a black rubber band over my shield number. The crackhead doesn't know any better. He is more terrified of being robbed of his crack than going to jail. We make him go back and knock on the door while we hide on the side. It's not unusual for a customer to come right back to buy some more. When they open the door for him we rush in. My badge is dangling and my gun is drawn. Trent has everything that I have except a gun. I put my gun to the chest of the guy that opened the door and Trent goes into all the other rooms yelling out commands as if he's a real cop. We keep everything happening so fast that the dealer doesn't have time to notice we're not cops. He's with a girl high on drugs passed out on the couch. Everything is happening just like Trent said. I quickly flex-cuff the drug dealer and blindfold him. Then Trent comes out of the back with drugs and money and puts it in a plastic bag. I'm ready to go. The girl on the couch never wakes up. I make sure that the dealer is cuffed tight and we head for the door. I peek out into the hallway first and when I feel it is safe, we head toward the stairway. Then, *POW!* a round hits the wall over our heads. I spin around and crouch on the floor, landing in a kneeling position like I was taught in the military. It's funny how shit comes back to you automatically when your adrenaline is flowing.

POW!

Another round hits the wall next to me but not even close. I see a figure holding a gun, peeking out of the door of the apartment next to the drug spot's door. My reflexes kick in and I return fire, letting off two rounds that hit the door as it slams shut. Trent hits the stairs and I'm right on his heels. When we exit the building I can hear the sirens of approaching police cars, so we decide to walk, not run, up the block to my van. I start her up and we're out. I drop Trent off after we split the loot. I got my money back and some product to make some more money.

When I get home I do my usual, which includes going through the mail. I see that I was approved for an apartment, so that means that I will be moving. I go to my room, take off my coat, and clean my weapon so that there will be little trace of its being fired. Without any remorse for what just happened that night, I sleep like a newborn baby boy in a powder-blue room.

CHAPTER 39

COPSTITUTE

Tink . . . tink . . . tink.

That was the sound that was coming from the utility closet in my housing area. I was in the officers' station watching over the inmates and watching out for Flocko and Officer Rains while they were gettin' busy. Recently Rains had come to me worried and complaining that it was getting too risky for her to be running around servicing these inmates, and she wasn't making enough money. I decided to help her out by implementing some of the ways that I made money in here. Her first customer was Flocko, due to the fact that he was being moved tomorrow to C-74, the adolescents' jail, in preparation for him to go up north to start his sentence. It was a going-away present for his being so loyal to me and helping me make this money. Rains was my meal relief for the day and as soon as my B officer went to eat, she and Flocko got busy. I had the other inmates glued to the television on both sides because I had put a porno show on the tube. I had my housing area hooked up where the DVD player had wires running from it to both of the TVs.

While they watched the DVD, I checked up on her and Flocko to make sure that he wasn't killing her ass in there. I cracked the door open a little and saw that he had her bent over holding on to some dirty pipes while he was on his tippy toes hitting it. I chuckled as I heard her badge keep hitting the metal pipes. That was what was making the *tink, tink, tink* sound. I told him ten more minutes and then I closed the door, knowing that he wasn't missing a beat. When they came out, I gave Flocko an inmate cup with some Hennessy in it and he went right to his cell and locked in. As a matter of fact, after the porno went off they all went to their cells and locked in, putting up the towels so they could make love to themselves in private.

When CO Rains came out of the utility closet she went into the bathroom to wash the dirt off her hands. She then came and sat down in the officers' station across from me and asked me how we were going to work this newfound business arrangement. I chuckled when she said, "Talk to me, daddy!" I was in the process of locking the remaining inmates in when I heard punches being thrown. I told Rains to buzz me inside on the floor because they were fighting. I went in on the A side, where I saw some inmates standing around and two other inmates rolling around on the ground. I grabbed the both of them and broke them up. They stopped immediately, so that's how I knew that it wasn't that serious. One inmate said, "Hey, I was walking to my cell and this lil nigga just clocked me, so I duffed him out." I looked at him like I didn't believe him and then he said, "On the real, Hey, I ain't got no beef with him, so I don't know why he clocked me." Then another inmate joined in and said, "Word, shorty been bugging like that for a minute now like he ain't got it all upstairs. So y'all better get him out of here before we kill him up in here." I looked at the other inmate and he just stood there with his arms folded. This wasn't the first time I'd heard of this particular inmate stirring up trouble. I figured that he was one of those "CO, I can't live here" kind of inmates, who would do everything they could to get out of the housing area. I didn't want to take a chance with him staying here and these fools doing something stupid to him, bringing heat to my housing area.

While everybody went to their cells I told the troublemaker to pack up his stuff. He put his sneakers back on—they had come off during the scuffle—and said, "I'm packed." I led him out of the housing area into the corridor next to the officers' station. Then I made a phone call to the "Movement" office, which handles where inmates will be housed. I asked if they could switch my inmate for another inmate from another housing area. I made the troublemaker, whose name was Jerry Lawson, sit outside until they came with the new inmate and the swap was made. I gave the new inmate my speech: "I'm going to give you half an hour to inspect your new cell. In that time if you find anything in there that does not belong to you such as a weapon or drugs I will let you turn it in to me with no repercussions. After that half an hour is up, if a search comes in here and finds anything that you're not supposed to have in there, it's on you." I then led him to his cell and locked him in.

I then returned to Rains to let her know how we could both make money. I told her that I had a bunch of loyal workers in here that I trusted. I'd set it up so that she serviced them, because they had been cleared through me. I'd provide her with protection and she would get her money up front. I was happy when she said that she and her girls would try my way out temporarily to see if it would work out. I knew it would, because I already had inmates in line with money in hand waiting for a chance.

Before I left that day I went to the back of my housing area where I could get a signal to use my cell phone. I saw that I had a missed call from a friend of mine, so I returned his call. He answered my call crying and saying, "Yo, Gee, what's good? I need you, fam." I asked, "What happened!?" Between sobs he said, "My Princess is gone, Gee. Them muthafuckas killed her!" I knew that he called his daughter Princess, so I asked, "What happened to her!?" He told me to get the newspaper, that there would be a story about a teenage girl being raped and killed by two men. I hadn't seen him or his family in a while but I did hear about that story. I didn't know that that was his daughter they were talking about. He said, "I need your help, Gee, because they caught them niggas and I heard that they are heading your way." I was angry because I knew that she was a good kid that got all As in school and everything. I responded, "Say no more. I got you, fam." When I got off the phone I went back to the officers' station and I sat back to think, saddened by what I had just found out. I was thinking to myself that right now I wore many hats up in this joint—drug dealer, contraband smuggler, pimp, and occasionally corrections officer—and now I'm just going to add one more to my résumé—hired gun.

CHAPTER 40

HOW DO YOU KNOW?

When I arrived the next day for work the jail was already on lock-down. All the chiefs and special investigative squads were swarming the joint. The upper brass personnel from all over the Island were there trying to organize the organizers. I fell in line, being the puny officer that I was. I just wanted to know what was the occasion for this much company in my jail so early in the morning. I stood against the wall in the corridor where we normally have roll call. I noticed the K-9 Unit coming through the gate accompanied by the Gang Intelligence Unit. I was standing there thinking that the last time I saw this much personnel all at once in the jail was when . . .

An officer next to me, talking loud, interrupted my thoughts and said to some other officers who were waiting that another inmate was killed last night. I knew that it had to be something serious. I was told to take my assigned post but to keep the inmates locked in because my B officer would be utilized in searching the whole entire jail. I heard all the higher-ups saying stuff like we have to take the jail back, these inmates are out of control, these officers are getting soft, and so forth and so on. I just chuckled a little because it was just like Corrections to rally up the troops after the fact and think that the aftermath effort was going to in any way stop the inmates from doing the same thing again tomorrow.

Here I was on my way to my post, which consisted of sixty inmates with no second officer. I went to my post and relieved the midnight officer, who was pissed because it was her kid's birthday and she had already been told that she was stuck on overtime and was not going home. After she left, I let Moe out. He was my lieutenant now that Flocko had left. He came up to the officers' station and we took care of business. He gave me the money he had made for me and the list of what my clients wanted. I had orders for coke, liquor, cell phones, and cooch. As I counted my money, Moe said, "That's wild what happened to ya boy yesterday, right?" With half of my attention, because I was busy adding and subtracting, I asked, "Who are you talking about?" He said, "I am talking about that Tobias kid." I looked up for a minute, trying to remember, *Tobias, Tobias* . . . Then I said, "Oh, yeah, you mean the kid from yesterday. What about him?" He said, "Hey, that's the kid that got killed yesterday." *Damn, I was just talking to that dude.* I could not believe that shit, I thought I was doing a good deed by getting him out of my unit before he got killed and he gets killed in the other housing area. Now I want to know how it happened. I wondered if he went over there doing the same shit that he was doing while he was over here.

Officer Z. Jones was the steady officer at the housing area where I sent Tobias. It was kind of ironic that a similar thing happened to her best friend Officer Bryant's watch just a while back. I had to find out what happened and I knew that when I went to meal I could get all the information I needed. If you want to know what's going on in the jail, just sit in the mess hall and it will come to you. I went straight there when I got relieved for lunch. The mess hall was packed. There were officers from other jails mixed in with officers from my jail.

Seating was tight but I managed to pull up a chair at a table with a few officers from my jail.

It took 1.2 seconds for the officers to start gossiping about what happened, each one with his own theory. The first officer said, "I heard that they jumped him and killed him when he was trying to take over the phones. Ya know that was a blood house." Another officer said, "I heard that Officer Z. Jones tried to stop them, then they turned on her." And back and forth they went.

"No, that was her steady house."

"I heard that they didn't jump her, just held her back so that she could not help the mate that was getting jumped."

In unison officers responded with "Ooohhhh."

Another officer/slash investigator said, "Ya don't want to know what I heard."

Then he just left that up in the air like he was dangling candy in front of a bunch of hungry kids, and like clockwork they bit, eagerly asking the attention seeker, "Yo, what did you hear? What did you hear?" Then he started talking like he was on prime-time television.

"Well, I heard that one of them broads was fucking that inmate, the head leader that ran that house. The mate that got killed was wilding out and disrespecting her, so the gangbanger sicced his goons on him to give him a beatdown and they overdid it by killing him."

Dead silence followed that statement, each of them trying to fathom the reality of that. I spoke out in disbelief, "Nah, dogs, I know those officers up there. They're not like that. All three of them are stand-up officers, and we all know that Officer Green don't take any shit and she will knock an inmate on his ass all day." They all looked at me, some in agreement, some just still in their own thoughts. Another officer gave his professional analysis: "I heard that he was MO. That's why he was acting a fool and they jumped him." Another officer asked, "How can you tell that an inmate is a mental observa-tion inmate? All these fools have problems. Some fake it just to get a lesser sentence. Besides, it ain't our job to diagnose whether a mate is sick in the head." I responded, "Well, all I know is that inmates lie on their dick all the time talking about they screwed this female CO or that one. So if ya ask me that's a lie." Then another female officer asked me, "How do you know?"

CHAPTER 41

MOM DUKES

"I'll see you later," said Officer Zepa. She was another copstitute who Officer Rains put on our team. The deputy warden had just pulled away and he and Zepa would be heading out to do their thing at a hotel in New Jersey.

The routine was that she would travel to my neighborhood and park her car next to mine. She wanted a witness who she would leave with in the event something happened, and I could be that witness. Apparently, the deputy warden had just received some money from one of the pyramid schemes that had recently swamped the Corrections Department (illegal or not, officers were getting paid from these schemes).

Officer Zepa and the deputy warden pulled off just as my friend Trina came and got into my van. She was my Western Union connect who would receive the money from an inmate's family. She came to drop off some money that she had picked up for me earlier. I gave her her cut and as she was leaving she told me that she cooked and that I could come get a plate. I told her maybe later because I knew that I still had to go to LeFrak City in Queens and then to Brentwood, Long Island, to pick up money. I was about to pull off when my phone rang. It was Officer Bryant.

"What's good, sis?"

"Yo, I heard what happened to my homie and I am on my way to her house right now."

"Yeah, that's messed up."

Then she went on to say, "I knew that God put me through what I went through when this happened to me for a reason, so that I could be there for somebody else. I know she's messed up right now because I was. You know they gave me three-quarters pay and disability, right? So I am no longer an officer." "No, I didn't know that," I answered. She continued, "Yeah, that inmate getting killed messed me up. I couldn't sleep. I kept seeing his face over and over again. It was crazy. The very thought of me having to go back into a jail again gave me anxiety attacks, but you know Corrections fought me on it tooth and nail. They tried to make me go back to work and all that but the minute I went inside the jail I was brought out by an ambulance stretcher." I said, "Damn!" Then I asked, "What ever happened with your case?" She said, "When it came down to it, Corrections had to admit to making some mistakes and Fran lost his job but nothing happened to King." I said, "That's a messed-up situation." Then she said, "I am on my way over to her house. So come through." I said, "Okay, but I have to make a run first."

I was about to pull off when my phone rang again and it was my moms and she asked me, "Where are you?" I said, "I am in front of the projects. Why?" Then she said, "You need to come up here and talk to your son." I responded, "I can't right now. What happened?" She responded, with authority, "You need to come noooow!" I was quiet for a moment, then I said "Alright" before hanging up. *Who does she think she's talking to? Hollering at me to come upstairs like I'm a little kid asking her can I stay outside and play. Shoot, I'm a grown ass man and I'm going to take my time getting up there, too.*

—

I ran into the building wondering what was going on that was so urgent. When I got inside the apartment I saw my son putting a whole stick of butter in a frying pan to cook a grilled-cheese sandwich and I noticed my mother standing in the living room with her hands on her hips. She said to me as I went to sit down, "Ya better git 'im before I do!" I said, "What happened?" She said, "He'll tell you." And then she stormed off into her bedroom. I turned to my son and asked him what happened. At first he didn't say anything. He just stood there bending up a perfectly good spatula trying to smash his sandwich in the frying pan. Then Moms came back into the living room and sat down and started watching TV (as if she was not listening to our conversation). I asked him again and this time he told me that he got kicked out of school for fighting. I asked, "Why did you do that and what were you fighting about?" He said that some kid had teased him about his sneakers in gym class, so he started fighting with him. *Is this what was so important, a little fight at school?* I looked over to my mother and she was looking right at me as if she was waiting to see what I was going to do. So I dared not act like making my rounds around the city was more important than this. I turned to my son and asked, "What's the matter with your sneakers?" He said, "They're old, Pop!" I said, "Didn't your mother just buy you new sneakers?"

And he said, "No, she won't buy them or the new video games I want."

"Why?"

"She's riffing about me not passing my classes."

"You getting into fights, getting kicked out of school, and you're failing classes!" Raising my voice, I said, "I can see why you're not getting anything. She's right. That's the way it goes. You don't do good in school, you don't get shit!"

Now my moms, aka Ironfist, chimed in, "That ain't all. He's back-talking his mother, too." I looked at him and said, "What I tell you about that?"

"I didn't talk back to her. All I said was that the fight wasn't my fault and she said that I talked back to her," he said.

I jumped up and yelled, "Who are you yelling at?" And he jumped up as well. I came around the table to meet him. He's fourteen and a little shorter than me and weighs about 270 pounds. I'm 290 pounds. Now I was pissed. This lil Negro was trying to man up. My moms jumped up to come between us and I put my hand up like, "I got this." I said, "What do you want to do? I see ya got those Q-tips at the end of your wrists all balled up like you're asking for something!" My moms got in my face from the side and started barking in his defense, "I didn't call you up here for this. How are you going to try and treat him like this now?"

Then she said, "You don't be around him enough to be all of a sudden beating on him."

I was bugging, looking at Ms. Ya-better-get-'im-before-I-do/come-upstairs-now like, "If you didn't want me to straighten him out then why did you call me up here?"

"What do you mean, I don't be around him?" I said. "This is my son."

She laid into me like she had been waiting for this day and had a speech memorized.

"You don't spend no time with these kids. All you do is come in and out of here all times of the night without a care in the world. Sometimes they're over here for days and you don't even know it. You claim that you be working overtime but I know better."

Then she mimicked me in what she thought was a manly voice, "This is my son!" She went on, "You don't even take the time out to get to know him but now you want to swell your chest up like you have the right to." *Why do I feel like I've just been set up?* I tried to come back at her by lying and saying, "I do be working overtime so that I could make up for the child support." Then I tried to switch the blame. "If his mother spent the money on my kids then he wouldn't have to be fighting over sneakers. I'm running around here working overtime and working outside security jobs trying to make it, so that's why I am not around." Moms was looking at me but I couldn't look her in her face because I knew that she saw right through me.

I focused back on my son, who's standing there looking at me, looking like me with his eyes beginning to tear up. I could tell that it was not out of fear but out of anger. At this point I didn't give a shit, because of the lashing that I had just received from my mother. I had to save face, so I tried to lay into him and said, "You're not a little baby anymore and you need to realize that I'm trying my best to provide for you and your sister. Don't nobody have any money to be throwing around every time you throw a tantrum about some damn sneakers and video games. You need to grow up and start taking responsibility for your actions. You need to stop being selfish and always thinking about yourself."

"I wonder where I got that from?" he said, and walked out the door.

Ooooh, I wanted to swing on his ass but I was stuck on stupid when he said that slick shit. I looked over at Moms, who was now back to pretending that she was watching TV. I could have sworn that she had a smirk on her face.

CHAPTER 42

IRON FIST

"Play your beds," I yell to the inmates, ordering them to get in their beds so I can make my rounds and count them to make sure that they are all here. I'm working in a dorm area on the midnight tour. I swapped shifts with another officer. I needed the shift so that I could handle some business.

After the tag team that I received from my son and my mother, I stormed out of the house to go pick up my money, then go to work. I'm at work drunk. I have the bottle in my pocket as I take count of the inmates. I want their asses to go to bed so I can sleep until my meal relief comes. Tonight I'm working with CO Patterson, who is the steady officer here. She's real quiet and so-so looking but her body is banging. She's sitting in the officers' station waiting for me to verify the count so that she can call it in. I notice that she has on glossy red lipstick. Besides it helping her look better, maybe she put on the lipstick to distract you from looking at her wandering eye. The eye didn't bother me none, because earlier while we were walking to our post I was behind her focused on the way her butt cheeks seem to have a mind of their own. I come back with the count, she confirms it, and I go inside the station. I'm feeling saucy, so I begin to joke around with her, hoping she'll laugh.

I compliment her on her hair and how nice she looks. I think she's opening up a little.

The captain comes and makes his rounds, signs the book, and leaves. Now I can pull up a chair and kick my feet up and get some sleep. As I'm close to dozing off, CO Patterson starts talking to me. She tells me that she has on makeup because she and her husband had gone out earlier. With my feet on the desk and my eyes closed, I respond, "You look good and he is a lucky man." She then pulls her chair next to mine and asks me if I really think that she looks good. I open my eyes and I see that she is a little upset, so I say with concern in my voice, "Yeah, why?" She tells me how she and her husband got into it tonight over a phone number on their caller ID. Apparently, it was a number that she dialed back and some woman answered. I say, "Sis, it looks like you need me." She looks at me confused, so I pull out my bottle of liquor. She laughs, saying, "Heeell, yeah!" She admits to me that she's not much of a drinker but needs one tonight. Not too long after, CO Patterson is as twisted as I am and becoming more and more comfortable with me.

She begins cursing her husband, getting louder and louder with each comment. Before I know it, her chair is right next to mine and her head is on my chest. She's talking about how she has to go the extra mile to keep her body in shape. Not looking directly at her, I tell her that I don't see a problem with it. My comment must have made her feel better, because she starts kissing me.

Now, I didn't come here tonight to get some cooch, but I should have realized the signals all along. Anytime a woman starts talking about her relationship with her man to another man, the door is opened. Add a little low self-esteem, and you are pretty much in. What sealed the deal with CO Patterson was the combination of liquor and ignoring the wandering eye.

We're kissing for a while when she stops. She's breathing hard and she tells me that she doesn't normally do this. I don't care what she normally does because I'm at attention. I get up and tell her to go in the bathroom. I look around to make sure that the inmates are asleep, since we are in a dorm area.

Mental note: Inmates are never asleep. There is always one of them up watching you at all times.

I come trotting back to her with penis in hand. We are in the bathroom and she's on her knees giving me pleasure, but she is making a lot of loud grunting sounds. I stop her because I think that I hear someone coming. We agree it's no one and we continue, changing positions. She says, "I always wanted to know how it felt to have sex at work in jail. I mean, I heard some other female officers talk about it but I never did it."

I bend her over the toilet because the bathroom is small and the sink takes up too much room.

I'm hitting it and just getting into a groove when she starts crying. I stop and ask her, "What's up? What's the matter?" Mind you, I'm still inside her. She continues to sob and tells me nothing is wrong and to keep going. She don't have to tell my drunk, unprotected ass twice. So I do my thing.

When we finish, she just collapses on the bathroom floor, in the fetal position, with her pants around her ankles. I don't know what to do, so I try to help her up and she tells me to leave her alone. She says that this is not her and that she never cheated on her husband before. I stand there looking like, "Hey, that's between you and him." I wipe myself clean and walk out of the bathroom. Just then, there is a knock on our area door. It's the meal relief and she's right on time. I knock on the bathroom door and tell CO Patterson that I'm going to meal. She tells me to go ahead and that she's okay.

———

I make a phone call to check things out. It's a go.

I'm not that drunk anymore because I sweated out some of the liquor. I walk at a quick pace to the other side of the jail, the cell side. I get to my destination and my homie, Officer Leslie, lets me in.

He says, "You got fifteen minutes before my B officer arrives. So make it quick." Then he hands me his black leather gloves with metal plate inserts sewn in them.

"Okay, cool. What cell is he in?"

"Eighteen. Use the stick to crack open his cell so that it won't make as much noise as if we did it electronically."

I walk down the corridor and I put on the gloves. I had been waiting patiently for this opportunity and now here it is. I make sure that I have tape over my shield so the inmate can't see my badge number. Then I crack open his cell. He jumps up, scared. Too late to be scared about anything; he had to know that in some way, shape, or form this was coming.

I hit him in the gut and he goes down and curls up on the floor trying to protect himself. I don't let him off that easy. I hit him as hard as I can in his ribs and his back. He yells out for help. I'm meticulous and not in a rush. I remember CO Leslie saying no face shots. I pull on his legs to straighten him out so that he can take this ass-whipping like a man even though he can receive a hundred of these and they will never add up to what he did. He begs me to stop and then covers up his face, leaving the rest of his body exposed. So I make him pay. As I rain down on him I let him know why I'm here. "You like to rape and kill little girls, huh? She was only four-teen!" *Thud!* A punch to his ribs, then another to his arm. With these gloves on I don't care where the punch lands because I know each one hurts. Now he is stretched out on the floor and he says, "It was a mistake! I am sor—"

I don't let him finish. *PYOW!* A punch right in his face, busting his lip. I can't resist. I have to, all the anger that I am feeling about what he did to my man's daughter just comes out of me. He knew, coming to jail with his charges, that this was only the beginning of his treatment. He knew just like all inmates know that this was jail justice for what he did. As he lies on the floor I say to him, "If I hear about this from anybody, you know that I'm coming back, and if I don't get you somebody else will. There is nowhere for you to go where I can't get to you, be it by officer or inmate. Do you understand?" He nods, then I tell him, "When you go to the clinic you know what to say." He nods and says, "The shower."

CHAPTER 43

BLACKMAIL

Two months later . . .

It's 7:20 a.m. and again I arrive to work late. I'm tired because I finally popped my mother's titties out of my mouth and started standing on my own. I was up late last night moving the rest of my stuff into my own apartment. I walk through the gate and the roll call captain calls me over to her and asks me to help another officer escort some inmates from the intake area to a housing area near mine. I was going that way. I am okay with it because at least I won't be marked late. I get inside the intake area and as usual it's total chaos. You have inmates coming from court, going to court, or inmates who are fresh off the bus getting ready to be housed. I'm standing there watching a rookie officer try to quiet down the new inmates so that he can call out their names. I hear him say, "Excuse me, can I have your attention? Can you please be quiet for a moment?" I shake my head, then step up and yell, "Everybody, shut the fuck up." They quiet down to a mumble. I yell again, "I don't want to hear shit! Keep your mouth shut or I will shut it for you!" Corrections training 101: Always make an example out of one of them. I pick a herb who is still mumbling under his breath. "You, stand up. You have a fucking problem!?" I do this to show the rookie officers how to set the tone for these inmates, and to let the inmates know how their stay here is going to be. The inmates quiet down completely when they see the other officers assemble behind me. The new officer steps up and starts to call the names.

We are in the corridor on the north side when two inmates break out into a fight. I order the other inmates to face the wall and I take off to go break up the fight. Brawling are two of the littlest inmates that I have ever seen. I separate them. Then order them to put their hands on the wall. One of them is Spanish, with teardrops tattooed under his eye. I'm cocky when I tell him that if he takes his hands off the wall I will take it as a sign of aggression and beat his ass. I turn to tell the new jack to subdue the second inmate involved in the fight and I hear something like nails scraping against the wall. The next thing I know I'm looking up thinking that the pair of black Timberland boots floating past my face look just like . . .

I black out.

When I come to, I see the officer wrestling the inmate that hit me. The inmate is looking at me, laughing. He says, "I'll dance circles around you, fatboy." I regain my bearings and go over to assist the other officers who've arrived on the scene to help out. After everything is over, I go to the clinic, because the new officer swore that I slipped while fighting this one-hundred-pounds-soaking-wet inmate. I go with that story because I am not about to admit that my big ass had just got knocked out. No, no, no, no, no!

I finally get to my post to relieve the officer that was there. I let Moe out and we do our usual. Then he tells me that the dude that I beat up the other day is running his mouth. I look at him like, "What dude?" And he gives me a look like, "Come on now, this is me you're talking to." The fact that he knows about it is not good. I ask him how he knows about it. He tells me that he talks to the inmates in the housing area where this dude is and they say that the IGs (inspectors general) had come to see him more than once asking about his injuries because they don't believe that he slipped in the shower. He heard that the dude described an officer that looks like me. I feel that if they knew it was me they would have paid me a visit by now. I tell Moe to send someone down there a pack of Newport cigarettes to shut him up or at least remind him of what I told him. I walk with Moe back to his cell and watch him communicate with the inmates below us by way of kite. I watch him tie a string around a pack of Newports and lower it out of the window. He gets a note back saying that my message will get sent tonight during their recreation time.

I go back to the officers' station when my B officer arrives. I let out the rest of the inmates and I have begun my daily paperwork when I hear a familiar voice say what's up to me. When I look up it is Trent.

Shocked, I ask him what happened and why he's here. He looks at me with a stone face and says in a low tone, "You know why I'm here," and walks off toward his cell. I don't know what he's talking about, so I go to his cell to see what's up. I order all the inmates to go to the dayroom and get out of the corridor so I can speak to him without anyone overhearing our conversation. I post up in front of his cell and ask him when did he get here. He says, "Last night." So I ask him again, "What happened?" He looks at me with a real serious look on his face and says in a low tone, almost a whisper, "Gee, you don't know why I'm here?" I look back at him, confused and curious, with one eyebrow raised. I say, "No, I don't." He takes a deep breath, then shakes his head and says, "Somebody snitched me out on that drug spot that me and you hit up."

I'm at a loss for words and panic immediately comes over me. A million scenarios enter my thoughts. None of them could make sense of how this could happen or who could have snitched on him. I look up at him and he's staring at me as if he's waiting for a response. I tell him I didn't do it and he gives me a look like, "Who else could it have been?" Then he goes and sits on his bed and says, "I don't know, Gee. I ain't going to take this ride by myself. They asking me who my partner was and all that." I'm stuck. I try to absorb what he just said and what exactly that means for me. I look at him, he looks at me, and then he throws his hands up in the air. Then he looks out of the window and says, "There is this lawyer that's really good but I need some help getting him. I don't have enough cash, so I need some help."

Then he says, "I don't know what's going to happen if I can't get some help." Now I'm looking at this fool sideways. *You get locked up. You suggest that I snitched on you to make me feel guilty that you're in here, and then you hit me with the need for money for a lawyer!* I sum all this up and come to the conclusion that this fool is trying to extort me. I say to him, "Look, I didn't snitch on you. I don't have anything to do with why you're here and I am not giving up money like that. Period!" He gets up from his bed and says, "Well then, get used to these cells."

CHAPTER 44

FELONIES

I'm heated. I'm nervous. I'm scared.

I feel I have to do something about this Trent situation. I get off work and retrieve my weapon from the arsenal. I go outside and get on the route bus, but before the bus takes off, the 3:00–11:00 p.m. tour captain gets on the bus. She claims she needs someone to stay for overtime. Out of everybody on the bus my name happens to be next on the list.

I reluctantly get off the bus, but before I go to my post I detour back to my locker and start sipping and thinking about what happened earlier. *I can't let this muthafucka extort me. How did he get caught and not me? Are they going to eventually catch me, even if he doesn't tell them?* Damn, I am messed up right now. The more I think about Trent, the angrier I get. That fool knew the risk just like I did. I took a chance with him and now he's trying to make me pay. Hell no, I'm going to deal with this dude tonight.

I go upstairs to take the corridor post. I'm a little intoxicated when my meal relief comes. He tells me to take my time because he's bored and just waiting to go home. So I head down to the officers' kitchen. When I get inside, there is a small group of officers sitting at a table watching television. I see Officer K. Johnson, one of the three amigos. She's leaning back in her chair in a relaxed position. I say to her, "It's weird being here without both of your partners, right?" Officers Bryant and Z. Jones are both out due to two separate inmate killings. She just nods at me as I walk past.

Then I hear her ask one of the officers sitting nearby to wake her up when it's time to go back to their posts. I sit down a few tables away from them and try to shake this feeling of nervousness. I'm close to dozing off when I hear an officer tapping Johnson on her shoulder to wake her up. It is time for her to go back to post. The officer shakes her gently while calling her name, but she's not responding. Now a sense of urgency comes over the officer as she frantically tries to get Johnson up. Other officers come over to assist.

They determine that she's not breathing. The officer who came over first to wake Johnson now gets on the phone and calls the clinic while the others lay her down on the floor and begin CPR. I get up and come over as an officer does the procedure. Under my breath I'm counting with him, "One one thousand, two one thousand . . ." The clinic staff arrives and takes over while the rest of us officers stand by watching and praying.

I get out of the way and watch the scene from a distance, as I know all too well from my military training, from my experience in here, and most of all from my experience with death in the streets that it is already too late. Officer K. Johnson is gone. Officers start crying. Then everyone is asked to leave until the ambulance arrives. I'm distraught. I can't believe what just happened. I go to my locker and sit and think about Johnson. She, along with Bryant and Jones, broke me in on this job, taught me the dos and don'ts. She was a very good officer and, most of all, a good person. She did her job by the book at all times and you never heard of her getting involved with any of the BS that goes on around here. I think about the three amigos and about life in general. It's crazy to me how all three of them are no longer here. I know that when her partners find out, they are going to be devastated.

I retreat to the locker room. I'm there by myself, replaying what just happened in my mind. And I'm sipping. Some officers come in and without a word being said pull out cups and join me. After a while it's time for me to go home. My tour is over and I am real tipsy. I'm on my way back to my post to log out when I remember Trent. I'm hurt because I just lost a friend, and angry because of what Trent's trying to do to me. As I stand up to leave my post I check myself to make sure that I am not leaving anything and that's when I feel it. *Oh, shit.* I must have rushed and forgotten to check my weapon. I had it on me the whole time.

I feel desperate and I need to get to Trent. I need to let him know I'm not just going to lie down for his shit. I make my way to my housing area and the officer, who is my steady relief, lets me in. She's crying because the news about K. Johnson has already traveled through the jail. I tell her that I'll stay and hold her down until her relief comes. She agrees because she is eager to go and find out about what happened. The inmates are already locked in for the night and all the lights are cut off.

I know that I didn't have much time to get at Trent. I go to his cell. I flash my light in there and see that he's asleep. I take the bar that we use to open the cells manually and open his cell as quietly as I possibly can. I stand over him as he snores. I take out my gun that I had forgotten to put back in the arsenal from earlier when the captain pulled me off the bus for overtime. I tap him on his forehead with my weapon. His eyes open wide when he sees me and he's about to yell. I quickly put my gun in his mouth so that he'll stop and see that I'm not fucking playing. I see sheer terror and disbelief in his eyes as he looks at me. I'm stone-faced. I put my finger up to my mouth, indicating that he should remain quiet. He nods. I pull my gun out of his mouth and he takes a deep breath. I look at him in his face and with a cold, calm, nonchalant attitude I say, "Do you still want to play this game with me? I commit felonies every day in here and in the streets. So do you think I'm going to allow you to come in here and fuck up what I worked so hard to build and just extort me like I am some lil nigga? Huh!?"

I raise my gun and put it on his forehead. He tears up and he has the not-knowing-what-to-expect-next look on his face. I say to him, "Don't fuck with me, Trent, because if I pull this trigger, your family might get some money but you won't know it." He looks at me, terrified, and tears are rolling down the side of his face and he stutters when he says, "Gee, it don't have to be like this. I'm sorry for what I was trying to do. I only did it because I am fucked up right now.

"As for this bid, I'm finished. They got me red-handed for murdering this kid over a year ago. Me being here ain't got nothing to do with you." He looks at my face to see if I believe him or not. He continues, "I am serious, Gee. Check my file. It will tell you what I'm here for and it will show you that it has nothing to do with what we did." I put my gun away, realizing the time, and say to him, "I'ma let you rock this time, but you better ask around here about me because anytime I feel like it, you can be touched. And just so I can sleep at night, as long as you're here, one of my peeps is always going to be watching you. And I have your name and numbers, so I will always be able to track where you're at and touch you if I have to . . . remember that."

I walk out his cell, slamming it shut. I return to the officers' station when the other officer shows up. I leave, and on my way out I see all the officers are coming in for the change of tour and are just now finding out about Johnson's death. I don't stop to talk to anyone because I don't feel like answering a thousand questions. I get to my van and just sit there for a minute and reflect on my life. I feel as though I am too caught up in that jail and I am losing it. I question myself: "What the fuck did you think you were doing?"

CHAPTER 45

INMATE LOVER

A week later . . .

"Yo, Hey, one of your boys got into it last night in my area," an officer says to me as we line up for roll call in the morning. I give him a puzzled look like, "Why are you saying 'your boy?'" I ask him, "What are you talking about?" He says, "One of your homeboys, your mate, you know, one of the inmates that you're real friendly with." Now I look at him seriously, because he's trying to play me in front of all the other officers lined up for roll call. He continues to act a fool by saying, "Don't have shame in your game now, we all see how chummy-chummy you are with some of these losers in here." Other officers nod in agreement and he goes on, "I myself have seen you slapping five and shaking these nasty jerking-off twenty-four-seven inmates' hands. These muthafuckas are the scum of the earth and you be talking to them like they're your boys from the street." Another officer chimes in and says, "They probably are." I hear a few of the other officers chuckle. Then the first officer says, "These mates ain't your friends, they're just a bunch of lowlifes, especially the ones that keep coming back in and out of here like a revolving door." Yeah, those are the ones that I like; the ones that are too stupid to make it on the outside; the ones that will sit there and tell you that this is a good jail to be in, or that jail is better; the ones that know how to bid; that know all the rules, as if this place is their home. Yeah, those are my niggas and I mean that literally. My niggas! I step on their necks every chance I get to let them know that when they come through those gates I own them and that they are my property now.

"Those ignorant fools keep my mortgage paid and my kids' tuition paid. Hell, I wouldn't know what to do if they wised up and decided that their life was worth something and did something for themselves."

I stand there with absolutely nothing to say. He clowns me some more and says, "They're not your friends, and the minute one of them can bring you down he will. You're my boy, but the shit that you do with them is stupid, and we see it, so stop being so dumb with ya inmate-loving ass."

After roll call I'm about to head to my post when I'm stopped by Officer Patterson. She asks if she can talk to me for a minute in private. I'm wondering why she's here because I normally work the three-to-eleven tour. When we get to a place we're secluded, she tells me that she purposely got her tour switched with another officer so that she could catch up with me. I give her a look of concern like, "What's so important that would make you do that?" She explains that she didn't know how to tell me this, but ever since that night that we made love in the bathroom she and her husband have been inseparable. As a matter of fact, when she got off work that night he was home apologizing with a dozen roses. They made love all night until the morning. I'm happy for her but what does that have to do with me? I never said that I wanted to be her man or anything like that. She then says that this brings her to her point. I look at her like,

"Yeeess?" She continues, "I really don't know how to say this, so I'm just going to say it . . . I am pregnant."

Oh, shit, here I go again!

I look at her but I don't say a word. Her eyes begin to tear up and she looks at me, searching for a sign, a response, something. I just look back at her. I already know what I need to ask her and I know what I want her response to be.

"So what are you going to do?"

She puts her head down and begins to sob. I want to hold her but I catch myself, remembering we're at work. She says, "I'm going to keep it." My jaw drops.

"What?"

She says, "I don't know what to do. Things happened so fast that night and then with him the same night, so I don't know who's the father."

I just look at her, shaking my head. I don't know what to do or what to say. She starts talking again and says, "I can't get rid of it. My husband has been trying to get me pregnant for years and he came with me when I got my checkup, so he knows already."

I'm puzzled now, wondering how this is going to play out. I really don't need some jealous or upset husband beefing with me over this. She sees the worry in my eyes and she says, "The baby might be yours or it might not be. So I am asking you not to ruin my life by putting this out there. My husband would never understand and would probably kill me." I rationalize what she's saying. What if, at a later date, she decides to come after me for child support? Can I live with knowing that I might have a child walking around in this world and not know it? But what choice do I have. I'm scraping and clawing my life back together. I can't afford this kind of drama in my life right now.

So I tell her that I can deal with the situation if she can. Then she breaks out in happy tears and we hug—at that point it didn't matter where we were. She dries her eyes and we both take off to our post.

When I get to my post I go through my normal routine. Moe comes up and wants to talk to me. I'm okay with it, so we do the usual. He goes into the utility closet and I stand outside like I'm giving him orders on how to clean it up. He says, "Yo, Hey, I was in the pens yesterday coming from court and I overheard your name ringing bells in the jail. Some dudes from the dorm side are talking about you. They were saying how you're the connect inside the jail and how they got you on smash." I question him: "Out loud right there in the pens?" "Yep, and they had a crowd around them. So you know if I heard, some CO done heard it, too."

I begin to sweat and I feel a little panicked. A million thoughts are going through my head. I knew that this would happen sooner or later. Inmates can't keep shit to themselves. I'm surprised that I lasted this long. I had a long run mainly because Flocko was here fighting his case but now I've been put on blast by dealing with these other inmates.

Damn!

Either it was an inmate bragging about my hustle with him in order to make himself look important, or it was an inmate that I decided not to rock with who is mad about it. Either way, the word is being spread, and it ain't no telling who knows or how long they've known.

After our conversation I let Moe go back to his cell and I go back into the officers' station. My cell phone rings. It's Officer Rains. She tells me that she got some money for me and she gave it to Zepa because she's not at work today. Then she says, "Oh, yeah, I have to tell you something. I was in the hotel with Captain Rogers and when we finished this fool gets to pillow-talking about the jail and guess whose name came up . . . yours. He starts saying all kinds of shit that he heard about you and other officers in the jail. He said that he heard that if you want to get rid of all the drugs in the jail, get rid of Heyward. You know I backed him down, saying that he was wrong and that you don't get down like that, and guess what his smart ass said? If he can be in here tricking on me then that Negro can be in there getting money." I'm silent. She continues, "Hello, hello." I say, "I . . . I'm here and I hear you. I'll get in contact with Zepa. Thanks." And I hang up.

I can hear my heart is beating. I'm trying to take in the fact that the jail is talking. *Who else knows?* I have to shut this shit down right now. I get the phone call to bring the inmates in my housing area to the mess hall for chow. I make the announcement. They line up and I bring them down the corridor toward the mess hall. When we get to the door the captain tells me to hold them up and then he informs me that he will watch my house and for me to go assist the captain on the inside of the mess hall.

When I go inside, a new captain who I didn't know is having a hard time controlling the inmates. They are up talking and walking around, just doing whatever they want. Then two of them square off about to fight. The captain doesn't see me come in. I walk up behind her and the other officer just as she is about to press her body alarm. Then all of a sudden everything stops.

The inmates stop running around, the two who were about to fight stop and sit down. Then everything calms down. They're just mumbling among themselves. Some of them start pointing. The captain turns around to see what they are pointing at and all she sees is me. The inmates are now orderly and manageable. Some of them even say what's up to me, even some I've never seen before. With things under control I turn to go back outside to my house and the captain who kept staring at me asks, "Who are you?" I look at my badge with my name under it and say, "I'm Officer Heyward." Then she asks me again, more intensely this time, while she looks at me, then to the inmates, then back at me, "No! Who . . . are . . . you?"

CHAPTER 46

THE TOMBS

As the weeks pass, I'm stressing because the situation seems to be getting worse. I shut down all my hustles and I'm trying to be a model corrections officer but the inmates keep trying to pull me back in. I'm now being openly approached every time an inmate who thinks I am cool sees me alone. I feel that I'm handcuffed, and I can't bark on them like I want to for fear that an incident may occur that will bring attention to me, which is the last thing that I need right now. I see now how easily and how quickly inmates can make your name hot. I now have inmates committing offenses in the jail in hopes to raise their classification so they can get housed in my area. My area is notorious, and nobody in their right mind would want to be housed here. I'm petrified every time I see an unfamiliar officer at our roll call in the morning. I feel that everybody now knows what I've been doing and that it's just a matter of time before I'm arrested at roll call in front of everybody. How crazy would that be? What will my coworkers think? But I know they would need a lot of proof to just come and get me like that and I feel that I've covered my ass well by only dealing with certain individuals. Most of the inmates that I dealt with primarily have gone upstate and whatever I brought in has already been used, so there is no evidence to be found. The only way for me to feel safe is for me to get out of this jail. So I make a phone call to Assistant Deputy Warden Benson, whom I'd known since he was an officer. He made his way up through the ranks quickly and we remained good friends. He had connections.

He tells me that he can help me but doesn't know how soon it can happen. I feel a little relieved because if I can make this move I can put all this stuff behind me. A week or two goes by and I get the notice that I'm transferred. I clean out my locker, say farewell to my friends, and on the way out the door I see an invite to the jail to attend Officer Patterson's baby shower. I think I'm going to put that behind me as well.

I get assigned to a jail called the Manhattan House of Detention, aka The Tombs. I feel relieved, like I just had a narrow escape. I feel energetic and alive, like I have a new start in life. I take my folder to the personnel office and that's when the bullshit starts. My transfer states that I'm to be placed in the courts part of the jail, where inmates are housed who have an upcoming court date. The thing about the courts is that it's unofficially reserved for officers with at least fifteen years' experience. The personnel office was questioning how I got the post with only nine years on the job.

The officer calls my connect and gets verification that I should be in the court part of the jail and not where inmates are housed. This new jail is real laid-back, and as I adjust to my surroundings I learn that everyone in here is here by way of a hookup or has fifteen years on the job or better. I get assigned to the search post, which of course is the worst post in the jail. I receive some disapproving looks from the officers there. It is clear to me that many of them are wondering how I got into the courts, or thinking that I must know somebody, or better yet, that I was sent from the inspector general's office as a spy.

At first I'm treated with a long stick and everyone is uncomfortable around me, until, of course, they need a person with my expertise. Several times out of spite I would be assigned a post on the jail side. I would be told that they were short staffed and with the least amount of time served, I was the right person for the job. It didn't bother me because even the jail side of The Tombs was less chaotic than my former C-73 unit.

One day I'm sitting down having my meal when a captain approaches me and asks me, "Are you the new officer from the Island?" I answer, "Yes." He says, "Come with me. We have a problem in the courts." It's been a long time since I was placed on the goon squad, but since I'm the new guy here, I should've seen this coming. We arrive at the staging area and I see some over-the-hill officers suiting up, getting ready to extract an irate inmate from a section in the courts. I chuckle to myself as I see the officers showing their age and how unfamiliar they are with the situation.

As they try and figure out how to put on the protective wear, some of them look up and see me approaching. I can see the relief in their faces as the captain tells them that I will be the lead man on this. I quickly suit up and stand by while the rest finally get it right. We go into the court side of the jail. As we get off the elevator, I hear an inmate screaming at the top of his lungs, "We reeeaaady! We reeaady! Let's get it!" I stand at the front of a cell with a large Plexiglas-type shield that covers me from head to toe. Inside the cell the inmate continues to yell. The captain warns the inmate to stand down for the one hundredth time.

I can sense the captain is nervous. The over-the-hill mob behind me is scared and the camera girl designated to film everything can't get the lens off the camcorder. I shake my head at the inexperience that they are showing. The inmate is watching all this and decides he wants to take advantage of the situation. I see the fierce look on the inmate's face and then I decide to get serious because I'm the first one he will unleash on if we open the cell. While they figure out the camcorder, I see the inmate take off his belt, wrap it around his fist, and get into a fighting stance. I size him up and I know exactly what to do to end this whole ordeal. I tell the captain to open the gate. The inmate looks puzzled. I'm sure he's wondering how it is that I'm telling the captain what to do and why I seem so confident.

The captain hesitates to open the cell. Everyone grows silent at my request. The captain looks at the inmate, who is ready for combat, then gives me a look like, "Are you sure?" I nod and he opens the gate.

The inmate steps back with his left leg and plants his foot so that he can get leverage when we rush in. This is exactly what I want him to do. We don't rush in. Instead I walk in, which catches the inmate off guard. While he's confused I slam the bottom of my shield down on his right foot. He yelps and drops to the floor, screaming and crying in pain. Situation resolved. Inmate is no longer a threat.

The captain and the rest of the officers stand there with their mouths open. I walk past them quietly and go to take off my extraction gear. That day helps me a little bit because I no longer get posts on the jail side of the Manhattan House. I now get the shittiest post on the court side of the Manhattan House. A few days go by. I get assigned to do meal relief. I'm working in an area called "the pens." It's where we place inmates who are awaiting their turn to see the judge. It's a lengthy process, so the inmates that are placed in the pens are packed in there, some standing or sleeping on the floor, because there's not enough space on the little bench that's there. It is now feeding time and I order all the detainees to stand up. I was told that this was mandatory to ensure that they were all okay.

While I am conducting the feeding in my area, I hear a commotion coming from another area of the pens. I hear an inmate saying, "Oh, shit! Oh, shit," as they are quickly being evacuated from a set of pens across from where I am working. The officer that I had relieved comes back and assumes his post, so I go to see what the commotion is about. When the relocation of the detainees is done, I take a look inside the pen. There is an officer kneeling beside a detainee. He is an old homeless-looking man. Then he rolls him over. His body is stiff and his face is a purplish blue. The old man is dead. Apparently, he had been there for a while. As soon as I see this, I know that it's time for me to get out of the area because I don't want to deal with any part of this situation. I just got here. I hurry up and leave the area to go to my next meal relief, which was the front gate. I am just in time to see the mass confusion unfold.

Captains are running back and forth panicking, telephones are ringing, with chiefs calling to get information on what happened. Officers are scattering like I did, so they won't be involved. They know what I know, that someone has dropped the ball. The detainee who died should have been found sooner. I know that this is just another sad day of COs cutting corners just to make things run smoothly. The Manhattan House was no different from Rikers Island, because every CO knows that you can't run a jail effectively by going by the book. Nothing would ever get done.

A week or two goes by and I'm finally getting used to my new jail. I'm feeling that I dodged a bullet by getting off the Island. I arrive for the three-to-eleven tour and the roll call captain asks me if I had gotten hurt. I told him no, then he orders me to go see Deputy Brian and straighten things out, because he's short staffed and needs me to take my post ASAP. I say, "Okay," and I go to the deputy warden's office. I knock and he tells me to come on in and sit down. He holds a piece of paper in his hand and asks me, "Do you know what this is about?" I say, "No. What is this about?" He says, "You have been placed on modified duty." I just look at him, shocked. He takes a deep breath and says, "You are to turn in your badge and gun immediately." I'm unable to speak.

They have a captain escort me to my apartment, because I'd left the metal shield that was attached to my officer's hat at home. When she's about to leave, the captain just says, "I hope you get this straightened out." She drives away and I'm standing in the street in a blue jacket, a blue shirt, and blue pants. Just like that, I was no longer in a corrections officer's uniform.

CHAPTER 47

MODIFIED

It's two days later and I'm on modified duty. I have to go to the courthouse in Queens. I wear civilian clothes and I have an ID that reads "Modified." I'm still receiving my regular base pay minus any overtime. I report to the personnel office and I'm greeted by a female captain, who gives me the rundown on how things go in this jail. She explains that the part of the jail that once housed inmates is now closed and that I will be the elevator operator, taking officers from one floor to the next, because all the exits are locked and the only way to go from floor to floor was by elevator. After the rundown she asks me if I have any questions for her. I ask, "Do you know why I am here?" She tells me that she is never told why a person is sent here. She just supervises them while they are here. She then suggests that I try calling the union. I take my post and shortly after that I call the union. The only answer they could give me was that I was under investigation. What kind they did not know.

When I go home that night I try to figure out what they had on me that would make them modify me. I had escaped C-73 where everything happened. They never caught me with anything and all the drugs were used up and gone, so what could they possibly have? I wonder who could have snitched. The only inmates that I truly trusted were Flocko and later on Moe. I had been dealing with them for a long time, so if I was going to be busted dealing with them it would have happened a long time ago. It was nerve-racking day after day trying to figure this out. One time an officer who worked in the personnel office told me that officers come through here with a lot of problems. Some go back to work after being there for months and some lose their jobs. He also said that most of the time the officers who are sent there know why they're there, they just refuse to say. When he said that, I gracefully removed myself from the office. Once again I found myself walking around outside in a trance trying to figure out what they were going to do, how long I was going to be modified, and what they actually had on me.

I started to focus on my movements in the jail and the precautions I took to make sure that nothing could come back to me. I never touched the products barehanded, so that means no prints. I never got stopped at the front entrance with anything on me. No money from Western Union could be traced back to me at all. If someone was snitching it would be my word against theirs because there was no physical evidence. I thought about Flocko telling me about other officers that were doing the same thing. So I tried calling the jail to ask to speak to the officer that he told me about. I was shook by what I found out. That officer had not been seen in the jail in a while. Maybe he had been modified; maybe they had something on him as well.

As the days go by I try to live a normal life but I can't shake the nervousness that I have every time I go to work. When I would go see my mother she would ask questions like "Why don't I ever see you in your uniform anymore?" I would lie and say that I just didn't wear it today. I started praying to God every night to get me out of this situation. I even started hallucinating about the things that were around me. Like one time I go to the movies to see *Big Momma's House* number two and at the end of the movie Martin Lawrence faces the screen and says, "Not guilty." He was, of course, talking about the father in the movie, but my dumb ass thinks that it's a sign from God. I even sought out an officer friend of mine who I knew from the streets who also worked in the Security Department of Corrections. I told him everything that was going on and he told me what I thought was some reassuring information. He told me that a lot of times the IGs will set up an officer and try to catch him by using fake cocaine. So if I knew for sure that what I was dealing was real shit, then they were not involved. I felt a little better after hearing that, knowing that because I only dealt with certain inmates and their families, my product was the real deal.

CHAPTER 48

SHOW ME SOMETHING

A few months have passed and I'm beginning to wonder if the department has forgotten about me. I'm anxious to get this over with. I want to find out what I'm up against. It's about six-thirty in the morning and I'm already late for work when the door to my apartment is buzzed by someone downstairs in the lobby. Who would be ringing my bell at this time of morning? I press the intercom button.

"Who is it?"

"The police."

I buzz them in and scratch my head as I walk toward the bathroom, not paying the police downstairs any mind, because in my neighborhood the police will buzz anybody just to gain entry into the building. I have nothing on but my pants when there is a knock at my door. Confused, I go to the door, thinking they must have the wrong apartment, and I know I don't have any trouble in the streets. I open my door and six burly white detectives my size or better are standing there. One of them asks, "Are you Gary Heyward?" Still confused, I say, "Yes." Then a Spanish woman comes from around the corner and flashes her badge. She says she's from the inspector general's office and that they are not here to arrest me. They just want me to come with them to answer some questions about an investigation that they're conducting. I agree. When I go to close my door so that I can put on the rest of my clothes, one of the police officers puts his foot on the door so that I can't close it. Another comes into my apartment and follows me to my bedroom, and watches me as I get dressed. I know then that this is more serious than what they are telling me, because they are treating me as if they heard that I was armed and dangerous. After I put on my shirt and shoes, one cop asks me if I have a weapon in the house. Before I can answer, the Spanish woman says, "No, we took that away from him already." I then ask, "Am I going to need the union or a lawyer for this questioning?" Her response was "We just want to show you something."

Show me something?

I leave with the officers and I get into an unmarked car. When we arrive downtown I'm asked to wait in a room while they prepare for me. As I sit there with four of the six officers right there with me one of them asks me, "You really don't know what this is about?" Nervously, I say, "No." Then the Spanish officer comes into the room and announces that they're ready for me now. Inside the room there is a projector at one end and a screen mounted on the wall at the other end. I sit down on one side of the table and she, along with an older gentleman, sits across from me. Then the older gentleman gets right to the point. "We brought you down here to give you a chance to help yourself." I look at him, confused. Then the Spanish officer says, "Take a look," and clicks on the projector. I look up at the screen as the video comes into view. My heart sinks at what I see. I begin to break out in a cold sweat as the video plays. I notice their attention is on me and my reaction and nothing else. I'm speechless as I watch the video of my big black dumb ass getting out of my van and standing right in front of a car that clearly has a camera crew inside it. They were videotaping my whole conversation and drug transaction. They ask me repeatedly if it's me in the video. All I can think about is fellow officers telling me that these inmates are not your friends; they will give you up in a heartbeat. I didn't believe those officers. I trusted the inmates I was dealing with. When they didn't get a response from me, they began to ask me, "Who else was doing it with you? You could not have run all of that by yourself."

The one person that I least expected, the one person who had been there with me from the beginning, and who treated me like a brother in the streets and in jail, had set me up. I mumble to myself, "I knew his whole family." Then I look up at the screen at me and Flocko's sister as the officers continue to ask me if that's me on the video, as if they really need confirmation, as if it isn't obvious. My throat is completely dry and in a low voice I ask for my lawyer and union rep. They tell me that I can call both. But they ask me again if it's me. I just ask for my lawyer, never admitting that it's me, Dumb Donald, up there on that screen.

Little did I know at the time that they did not need me to admit that it was me, because there was a hidden video camera inside the room filming my reaction. They tell the police to come into the room and arrest me. I'm asked to stand. They search my pockets and place handcuffs on me. Then the Spanish officer says, "Well, we gave you a chance to help yourself. If you had told us who else was doing it with you then we could have helped you." My street sense takes over and I feel deep down she is lying. They were going to arrest me no matter what. The truth is, even if I was being helped I would not have said a word.

For the very first time in my life I feel the cold steel of handcuffs on my wrists. A chill comes over my body and a million thoughts run through my head.

What's going to happen to me?

CHAPTER 49

HOW THE FUCK DID THIS HAPPEN?

When they first put the cuffs on me I was inside a room but now I am being escorted out of the building like a common criminal. I can hear people talking about me. I see them staring at me as my head is being ducked down into an unmarked car. They are taking me to the Bronx Criminal Courthouse on the Grand Concourse. It's a silent ride.

At the courts, I get fingerprinted and they take my mug shot. It seems surreal having the arresting officer take my picture, telling me to face left so that they can get my side profile. Then they place me in a small holding pen and handcuff me to a pole that lines a wall. There are other detainees in the pen, too. They have no clue who I am.

After I'm processed, I'm taken upstairs and turned over to the corrections officers that run the pens there. I am greeted by an officer that I know. He tells me to have a seat on a couch that is placed in front of a desk. He asks me if I am alright and tells me that they were told that there are more officers who will be arrested. He felt that what was happening with me and the other officers was some bullshit political move that the department was on. I'm sitting there and one by one others arrive. Among them is the other officer I had been searching for earlier to find out what they had on me. He comes in and sits down. Our eye contact says it all. We both know that we we're up shit creek.

The corrections officer lets me use the phone to make as many calls as I want. I call my best friend and tell him what happened. I tell him not to tell my moms because I didn't want her to know anything. I could always make up a story to her if it was just about me losing my job. I want to wait until after I see the judge to do anything. I didn't think I was going to get locked up. And I didn't want my mom worrying about me.

A union lawyer then shows up. He's livid about how we've been treated. To him, the charges aren't that serious. With all the legal jargon that he is spitting out about how our situation is bogus, still there is nothing he can do to stop us from getting locked up. A female captain comes into the area and tells the officer on watch that we can't sit here, that we must be placed in a holding pen. We all get up and march to our respective one-man pens. The officer that I know gives me a sad stare and the captain locks the pen.

"Yo, bigman!" a detainee, soon to be inmate, yells out to me.

I'm deep in thought, so I ignore him. Really I'm in shock. I can't comprehend what is going on around me. My chest tightens, my breathing becomes shallow, and my brain feels like it's too big for my skull. Again, "Yo, bigman! Why you in here, bigman?" Getting no response from me, the detainee asks a passing corrections officer, "Yo, CO, why he gets to be in a pen by hisself and we gots to be packed in here like sardines and shit? Who the fuck is he, the president?" The officer just looks at me with disgust, shakes his head, then turns to my tormentor and says, "Shut the fuck up before I give you something else to worry about besides being sandwiched in." The officer glares at me. All I can do is put my head down.

I have just finished being processed and I'm waiting to see the judge. And what I think is going to happen, doesn't. I thought that because I was a corrections officer, the judge would let me go on my own recognizance so that I could fight my case from the street.

Instead, the DA gives a speech that makes me look worse than Saddam Bin Hussein Laden. She hits the judge with all sorts of hideous and heinous acts and shit. She's all upset about me being uncooperative (not snitching) and shit. *Da fuck!* By the way she is describing me you'd swear that she's referring to a guy who killed like thirty little kids or something. I lose count after the first five or six charges. I just keep looking at the judge, shaking my head.

During the arraignment I look over my shoulder and I see her. Moms. We make eye contact and I crumble. My heartbeat is getting louder, blocking out whatever is being said about me. She looks supportive. She also looks embarrassed, humiliated, and pained. I want her to see that I'm sorry. I didn't want her to come here to find out about me this way. I want to say so many things that will comfort her, something that will make the pain go away. But I can't. I'm instructed to face forward.

That is when I hear this front-page-grabbing, charge-exaggerating, I'm-bucking-for-promotion-on-this-nigga's-black-ass bitch say, "Your Honor, we are asking that the bail be set at one hundred thousand dollars." I look over at this crazy bitch and say, "You buggin'!"

I shake my head frantically. I look back at my sister, who accompanied my moms. She looks shocked. I can hear my cardboard cutout of a lawyer argue to get my bail reduced, but all I'm thinking is *I'm sorry.*

I go back to the holding pen where my man, do-dirty (the detainee), has recruited a supporting cast. It's now a group effort to find out why I'm isolated. I ignore them. Then without warning I hear the television. It faces the pens so inmates can see. The news is on.

"Three corrections officers and three counselors were arrested today on drug charges."

I turn to look up at the television. Right there, front and center, they have my picture plastered all over the tube. *No they didn't! No these dirty muthas didn't!* But, yes, they did. They have my picture up there blown up for the world to see as the report explains and exaggerates the story. I remember the newscaster saying, "Correction Officer Gary Heyward could be facing life in prison." *For a half ounce of coke!? Come on now, knock it off!* Then comes the coalition. I put my head down to brace myself.

"Ayyooo, bigman! You was doing it like that, bigman?"

Then one detainee to another, "Yo, son, dude was gettin' it." He and his backup dancers break out in laughter. I was the topic of discussion for the rest of the night.

"I bet it was a snitching-ass nigga that blew it up."

"Niggas don't know how to act when they got a nigga looking out for them."

I sat there thinking about my family, my kids. What will they think when they find out? *Damn, how the fuck did this happen?*

CHAPTER 50

THE TRANSITION

I was harassed by the peanut gallery all night until I was moved out of the Bronx courthouse. They took me and the other officer to a jail called the Boat, also located in the Bronx. It was actually a large floating barge. We were placed in a cell in the intake area until they figured out where we would go next. We sat in that cell for hours, rarely speaking. We overheard that he would be bailed out by his wife. I had no wife. I had no one to bail me out. I had no stash and nothing to show for all of the hustling. All the dirt I was doing was for nothing.

We were visited throughout the night by officers we knew. They consulted us and expressed that they thought the department was wrong for what they were doing to us. They gave us the benefit of the doubt. They believed that when we got exonerated we could sue the Corrections Department. When they left, I'd shake their hands but I couldn't look them in their faces. How could I? I considered these officers my friends, that I, on occasion, went into battle with. They taught me the job. They had my back. And here I was disrespecting everything that they stood for. They performed their duty every day but did not crumble like I did.

Eventually I got moved to the Nassau County Jail in Long Island. The officers there were giving me the benefit of the doubt and thought I would make bail and fight this from the streets. When I got there I was allowed the courtesy of placing a phone call. I prepared myself to do the hardest thing that I've ever had to do in my life. I called my moms. I hadn't talked to her since all this started. I remembered the look on her face in the courtroom. I knew that I had cut her deep.

I took a deep breath and dialed the number. Half a ring and I heard a hello. I could tell she had been up waiting to hear from me. I was sure she just wanted to hear that I was okay. "It's me," I said. She was quiet. Then she asked me if I was okay. I told her I was fine and she went right into talking about getting my bail money up. She told me she'd been filling out paperwork and that she would take out a pension loan from her job. She'd also contacted my aunt in Alabama about putting her house up.

I didn't want her to know that I was stressing. The same way she was being strong for me, I wanted to be strong for her. She was going so hard for me. But there was something I had to tell her. I had to hold my head up and not let her hear my voice crack. When she started to speak again, I stopped her.

"Ma."

She paused to listen. I hadn't said a word since she started telling me about her plans to bail me out.

"Ma, I did it."

Dead silence.

Don't crack. Don't break down on this phone.

I told her that I didn't want her to take out any loans for anything or do anything with anybody's house. I told her about how the child support payments were the reason I had made this bed. I told her that I would deal with everything myself. She was quiet. I could feel the added pain that I was causing her. I felt I had to admit everything because I knew that my mother would fight for me until the very end. I broke the silence by telling her when my next court date was and that I would be okay here where I was, and that I would call her as soon as possible. Then I said the stupidest thing that I could say to her. I told her not to worry, which I knew would make her worry more. When I got off the phone I got processed into jail.

I gave up the clothes that I had on in exchange for an orange shirt and pants. Written on my new shirt was the word "inmate." The transformation was quiet. The officers who escorted me weren't saying anything. I guess they felt awkward about escorting me. I was silent because of the shame I was feeling. It was a routine process for the officers but devastating for me as a new inmate. I kept my head down and my words were few. Just one-word answers when I was asked a question. I got searched and instructed to strip. I was ordered to open my mouth, lift my arms, and bend over, spreading my ass so that they could check it for contraband. I was given an orange pair of sneakers. The Timberland boots that I was wearing weren't authorized for inmates to wear in jail. I was then escorted to a cell. Inside there was a bed, a sink, and a toilet. I knew my surroundings well. I'd checked them things for weapons over a million times. I settled and I realized that I was tired. I'd been up all day, so I tried to get some sleep.

During the next couple of days I was kept in my cell for twenty-two hours out of the day, allowed out only to shower and use the telephone. I was fine with being locked in for now because I didn't really want to be around other inmates. I tried to sleep for much of the day because when I was awake all I could think about was how much time I was going to get.

The next morning a CO came to my cell and let me know that I had a visitor. I already knew who it was. I washed my face, brushed my teeth, and prepared to see my mother face-to-face. As I was escorted to the visitors' floor, I kept saying to myself, "Stay strong. Don't break down. She doesn't need to see you like that." When I saw her, I went over and gave her a hearty hug. We sat and began to talk. She told me that she was holding up okay and that she was concerned about me in here. I looked at her and said, "This is a fine mess that I have gotten myself into, huh?" She answered, "Yeah." She let me know that my kids didn't take the news well. She put her head down. I tried to convince her that I was alright and not to worry. But I was not sure it was registering with her. She looked up and told me that my story was all in the papers and on TV. I already knew but I hadn't watched TV since I'd been locked up. So I asked her, "What were they saying exactly?" She said, "They just be going on and on about the things that you did, the charges that they have on you, and the fact that you're facing life if convicted."

That last one kind of hung out there. We both didn't particularly care for the "life if convicted" part, so to ease her concern I said, "Ma, you know the papers make things up to hype up a story." She agreed with me but she was not convinced. My hour was up and my visit was over. We hugged again. She stood there looking at me until the door opened for me to go back and I disappeared into the jail.

When I got back to my cell I was wide awake and as usual thinking about all the stuff that had happened. I remembered when I got the letter to be a CO and how happy my mom was and how we danced around the living room that day. I thought about what it was supposed to mean for our lives. Then I thought about what she was going through, how my kids must be affected. If something happened to my family, what could I do for them now? I thought about all the things that I was trying to fix by hustling. But it didn't fix anything, it just made things worse in my life. Now my family was suffering, too. I then did something that I hadn't done in over twenty years. I didn't do it when my brother died or when my father died. I never really felt a need. That day, I sat in that cell and broke down and cried. It seemed like my body had wanted to for a long time. I just released everything. Tears came down my face as if I had opened the floodgates. For the first time in my life my big 290-pound ass was lying on the bed provided for me, in a fetal position, whimpering to myself like a little bitch.

CHAPTER 51

THE COPOUT

I'm going through it. Now I can't sleep. I'm staring at my reflection in this dull piece of plastic on the wall that's supposed to be a mirror.

Look at Gary Gee from the Polo Grounds projects . . . look at Big Gee the marine . . . look at Nutmo the corrections officer . . . now look at Gary L. Heyward, Nassau County Correctional Facility inmate.

I'm in my cell thinking about the possibility of life in prison when I hear a bang coming from the cell across from mine. I look up and see an inmate trying to get my attention. He points to his head, indicating that I hold my head up and that everything will be okay. He mouths to me that he was a Rikers Island CO and that he was going to request that we be put together for our one-hour recreation time. I nod "okay."

When recreation time comes, they let me spend it with the inmate across from me. A few other inmates are there, too. He tells me that his name is CC and that he was a CO on the Island who got caught up in a messed-up situation. He tells me that he's been here a minute but has a court date coming up and he's hoping that he'll be released.

We talk for a while and he gives me the lowdown of the jail. For the most part, the officers don't mess with you as long as you do what you're told. He tells me that he knew who I was from the newspapers and that the department was trying to railroad me by trying to give me life. I can't focus on that right now though. We'll see what happens when I go to court tomorrow.

Our one hour of rec time goes by fast and I'm back at my cell. I find out that I have a legal visit. I'm escorted to an office where a counselor from the law firm that represents the Department of Corrections is sitting. Very plainly he tells me that a jury has already indicted me. So if I try to fight the evidence, there is the undercover (which I think is Flocko's sister), the videotape, the voice recordings, and the inmate who is supposed to testify that I was running a major organization. Upon hearing this I am really feeling the pressure. I am shook. Then he says, "If you take the deal that I'm about to offer, you can make it a little less painful for yourself." My heart's pounding. Here is the moment of truth. I didn't know if he would say twenty-five, fifteen, ten years, or what. I take a deep breath and ask, "What is the offer?" He explains, "I know the DA on your case, and, not to make light of your actions, my office still tries to give the best representation that we can. So I pleaded with her saying that your job record was real good until now. I asked if she could go a little easier on you. As a favor to me, she said that she's offering two years. It's only on the table today; if you don't take it now we are going to start picking a jury for trial."

He just sits there waiting for my response. I'm quiet, thinking that maybe he has more to offer.

Two years? Two years? Maybe they don't have what they say they have? Fool, yo black ass is on that tape. You saw that yourself and if a jury sees that, how would you explain your actions?

He's still waiting for an answer.

"I'll take the deal."

When I get back from my visit I am moved into a cell with CC. I tell him that I'm going to take the two years. He's more relieved about it than I am. He thinks it's a great deal under the circumstances. He explains to me that since this is my first offense, it's possible that I could get into an early-release program like Shock (a military-style program that lasts for six months and then you go home) or Work Release (a program where an inmate can go out into the city and get a job by day and come to jail at night). For me, either one of those would be better than serving time upstate. To qualify for the programs you're rated by a point system. You get points according to what kind of citizen you were, if you've been in and out of jail, if you've held down a job, and if your crime was a violent one or not. You need more than thirty-two points. After tallying up my score I had forty-five. I'm feeling good about my chances.

I call my mother to tell her the news about my plea. She's not too thrilled that I agreed to take the two years. She feels that the jump from a life sentence to two years means that I have a chance to beat the case. I'm thinking two years is great given all the dirt I did. But she didn't know that. I also tell her about the different programs that would grant me an early release. She's not that interested in all that, she just wants to get this chapter of our lives behind us. Right before I get off the phone, she says, "Don't worry about me. You just do what you have to do in there to get out of there."

I'm back at my cell just in time for chow when I'm greeted by yet another CO, who wants to see the corrections officer who is locked up. I felt like I was on display sometimes. When they brought my food they'd come, look, and just stare, then make a comment. This time my food tray is thrown down on the table and the comment behind it is "Heyward, tell me, how does this food taste?" I don't respond, because I know that this is just the beginning of things to come.

The next day I'm taken to the city for trial and sentencing. I'm sitting in a holding pen waiting for my case to be called and I see several officers whom I worked with at one time or another. Some stop by to look at me in disgust, others give me a few words of encouragement. I really felt embarrassed and humiliated when officers whom I was close to would visit. All I can do is turn my head away. I just want this sentencing part to be over with so I don't have to come down here again.

An hour or so has passed when the judge calls me in. As I'm being led over to my lawyer, I see my sister and my uncle sitting there. My mother is not here. I see Officer Rains and Zepa, my copstitutes, on the other side of the courtroom. They're crying. I'm instructed to face forward and at this time I notice four officers, two corrections and two court officers, standing behind me. It would appear that I am some kind of dangerous person who warrants this type of attention. I just shake my head at the show.

The judge announces my name and asks if I understand the terms of the plea bargain deal in front of me. I answer, "Yes." Then he asks if I have been threatened or coerced into taking this deal and I say, "No."

"I am sentencing you to two years incarceration and one year postrelease supervision," the judge orders.

Before the judge hits his gavel, my lawyer says, "Your Honor, my client qualifies for the Shock Incarceration Program and was wondering if we could get that for him?" The judge says, "Give him Shock if it's available for him." I'm excited, because this means that I can finish the program and be home in six months. All I have to do now is just stay focused and get through this.

CHAPTER 52

BULL PEN THERAPY

Getting out of here in six months has lifted my spirits. I have a different pep in my step when I'm escorted down a corridor back to the holding pens. I am placed in the last pen by myself to wait for my ride back to Nassau County Jail. I notice that the pen next to mine has four people in it. One guy is facing the bars with his hands hanging through them. He is talking to another inmate in the adjacent cell. I can tell that they're gay by the nature of their conversation. The CO, as he escorts me, yells for them to keep it down. I sigh heavily because I know that I'm in for a long day of bull pen therapy. That's when Corrections has you sitting in the pens all day and all night, spitefully making you wait until you're the last one left before you're sent on your way.

Some time has passed when I hear a voice say, "He's back there, last pen." I hear footsteps, more than one person. I look up to see Officer Jackson, who I worked with before. I don't know the other officer. Jackson has a confused look on his face like, "Hell naw, not my dawg!" He asks me what happened. I can't face him. I put my head down. He doesn't let it go. "This ain't the Heyward I remember before I left that jail," Jackson says. "You was the fly uptown Negro from Harlem cracking all the jokes, getting the chicks, playing basketball, and all that, so what happened?"

I try to answer.

"The child support," I say. My voice cracks.

I figure he understands, since damn near every male officer is getting hit up for it. He goes in on me, saying, "You know what you've done to yourself? Yo, check it, people are busting their asses out there trying to be where we're at doing a job like this. This job has a lot of opportunities for people, especially people from the hood. You know they don't want us to come up like this. Look at the things we get with this job. We get benefits. Our family members get benefits, too. Can you imagine a muthafucka running around here with no benefits? Look at our job, hey. We sit around all day babysitting just in case something happens. That's all we do. And you fucked that up. Now that they done raised the bar as far as qualifications to get this job with that college or military shit, you got all kinds of people trying to work on the Island, crackers included. You have officers really doing it. I mean going to school, getting degrees, owning businesses, and all of that. Not to mention buying houses and really getting their families up out the hood. Now that's what this job is about! That's what you were supposed to use this opportunity for. Now look at you." I hear anger in his voice now. In a low tone he says, "Do you know how you're making us look as black people right now? All in the paper, all on the news. They're thinking, I told you that you can't give them nothing—look at this."

When he finishes he stands there out of breath and looks at me with anger and disgust. Then the CO who I don't know starts talking. "Six. I have six kids and I love my babies to death; that's why I couldn't do what you did. I've been through it all. I have child support right now. I have a restraining order against me that stops me from seeing my kids right now. I have not seen them in months and when I did get to see them it was at a police station with a cop standing there supervising. All of this because she said that I threatened her and them with my gun. Even though this incident that she claims happened, happened in a building lobby and the video shows that she's lying, they still will not let up off me because of my outburst when the judge still denied me visitation. Even though the evidence says she made it all up! Brother, my check right now is sixty-three dollars every two weeks. I survive off a second gig off the books. I see her all the time with her new man around my kids and it just hits me in my gut."

He pauses and I can tell that he's getting emotional just talking about his situation. He continues, "As an officer right now my weapon has been taken away from me and even though the Firearms Review Board knows that I didn't threaten her with it, I still may not get it back for years. I'm saying all of this to say that child support should never be an excuse. We took an oath to be an officer. We swore that we would do this job. All that stuff that Officer Jackson said you lost as far as the perks of this job is true, but in time you can get that back. The one thing that these inmates took from you that you may never get back is your integrity."

They stand there for a moment to see if they have done the damage that they came to do, to see if I absorbed what they were saying. The way that I'm feeling, I would have rather they just beat me. Then the other officer says, "You're a big dude, so I know Corrections used you in the past to whip ass and I hope you realize that it's a small world up north and that you will run into some of the inmates that you beat down, so I hope you know how to fight. There's a difference when you don't have one of us with you jumping one of them."

They leave and I don't say anything. I feel like a carcass that a pack of wolves has left after a feeding. I sit back and think about everything they just said while I wait for my ride back.

A few hours pass and I must have dozed off. I wake up hearing a scuffle going on in the pen next to me. It has something to do with the gay guy. I can't see it but I can hear it. I can barely see the expression of shock on the face of the gay guy across the hall. No one screams for the CO or nothing. Then I hear the gay guy say, "Nooo, stop it." He says it in a low voice as if he doesn't want to alert the CO. Then I hear another dude say, "Come on, maaan, you got to do that right here, right now." A third voice says, "Shut the fuck up. Gay or not, you're next." I hear a slap and a thud as if someone hit the floor. The gay guy in the pen across the hall says, "Don't fight him. Girl, he's gonna take it anyway." Then I hear a flopping sound and the gay guy moaning. I can't believe that this shit is happening right here in the pens! I look across to the other pen and the other gay guy backs away from the bars and out of my view. The rape goes on for about ten or fifteen minutes, then ends with the assailant taking a shit in front of everybody and the gay guy whimpering.

A short while later I hear footsteps and my name being called. It's time for my ride. As I get shackled and walk out of my pen, I look into the cell where the rape happened. I see the gay guy sitting with his head down, very close to another inmate. The other two are sitting away from them on the other side of the pen. No one says a word.

My sentencing and what just happened in the pen next to me give me much to think about as I sit in the van on my way to Nassau County.

CHAPTER 53

DOWNSTATE

After I spend two weeks at the Nassau County jail, I arrive at Downstate Correctional Facility. I have handcuffs around my wrist and shackles on my feet. I'm escorted inside by a city CO, who then turns me over to a state CO. My sentence begins at that moment.

A short CO grabs me by my arm after my handcuffs are removed and leads me toward a wall, then yells, "Put your fucking head in that wall and don't move." *Here we go.* I do what I'm told. Then the city CO that brought me up from Nassau pulls him over to the side and says, "He's one of ours." Then the state CO comes over to me, looks me in my face, then pats me on my back and tells me to hold my head in there.

They place me in a cell by myself. I'm there for hours and in that time I hear ass-whippings being handed out left to right. I start thinking about when I was the one dishing out the ass-whippings. Then I hear a CO say, "Put him in the cell with the big black guy with the big dick." My cell opens and a stocky white guy walks in. I recognize him right away because his face, like mine, was all in the papers. The "big black guy with the big dick" statement now makes sense to me. He's in here for a hate crime against black people. No matter where he goes from this point forward I know COs will give him their own kind of justice.

The holding pen that we're in is tiny. There's a bench, which is barely big enough for me. I can tell the white guy knows why he's in here with me. I'm black and twice his size. He stands against the wall on edge as if he's waiting for something to happen. *This is some bullshit. I don't need this and I hope this fool don't pop and try to fight me thinking that I want to do something to him.* I've seen this scenario what seems like a million times now. An inmate will start a fight with a stranger just to get moved to a different area. I decide to defuse the situation before it even begins. I say, "Check this out, I know who you are but you don't know who I am. I'm the corrections officer that got in trouble for hustling drugs inside the jail." He raises his eyebrow and lets me know that he's heard about me. I continue to ease the situation by telling him that I don't want any problems. I'm here to do my time and that's it. He nods and I move over as much as I can so that he can sit down. He tells me his name is Rick, but I already know that from the news. We don't speak after that. A few more hours pass and we're taken out of the cell to get processed.

They have us go through the whole thing together. We're issued our green clothing, which all inmates wear, and they give us everything else we need. Then a sergeant comes over to me and asks me to sign some paper saying that I want to be placed into protective custody. I refuse. Then he tells me to sit on a nearby bench while inmates arrive for processing. When it gets good and packed, he yells out, "Hey, Heyward, how long were you a corrections officer on Rikers Island?" Everyone looks at me as if I was E. F. Hutton. I stand up and look back at everyone that is looking at me and say, "For nearly ten years." All you hear after that is mumbling and pointing from the inmates. I know I'm going to have a rough road ahead of me. Then the sergeant comes back over to me and says that because the inmates now know who I am, I'm a safety hazard for the facility and they are placing me involuntarily into protective custody so that they can better protect me. I really don't want it, because I know that PC inmates are locked down for a large portion of the day, in some places for a whole twenty-two hours.

We go through more processing. The white guy continues to get harassed by the COs. They tell him to put his feet on the black line on the floor or put his fingers on the black ink pad to get fingerprinted, always emphasizing the word "black." Then we go to get our medical checkup. Six COs escort us to a large room about the size of a gymnasium. We sit on one side of the room. We're by ourselves, while on the other side about a hundred black inmates are getting processed. The looks and stares are crazy and with the number of COs escorting us, they know that we're high-profile. Rick is recognized right away. I can overhear some of their conversations. The CO orders them to stop talking. The inmates settle down, then the COs start talking shop among themselves. I look into the crowd across from us and I see a few inmates making hand and facial gestures toward me. They worked for me at Rikers. They bump their fists together, then mouth to me, "Hold your head." Some of the inmates who don't know are looking at me and putting their fists to their jaw like, "You know who that is?" I guess they're thinking that since I'm close to Rick, I should pound him out right now. I look at them, then look at the barrage of COs around me and Rick, then look back at them as if to say, "How can I?"

Really, I'm not even entertaining the thought of doing anything to anybody. I just want to get processed so that I can find out when I go into the Shock Program and get the hell up out of here. After we finish our processing, we're taken to our cells and locked in. Then one by one they let us out to use the telephone to call home. I call my moms and get yelled at. "Where are you?" I tell her and she calms down, because she knows this means that we can finally get some answers as to how long I'll be in here. I tell her that they told me the counselor will come by this week to see me. She tells me that she will be up here later in the week. We say "I love you" to each other and hang up. Then I can hear a voice recording on the line, "You are talking to an inmate incarcerated at Downstate Correctional Facility."

CHAPTER 54

EL STUPIDO

The next day, I go see the counselor assigned to me. I'm a little hyped because I'm hoping I'll find out how long I'm going to actually be in prison. The counselor sits me down and goes over my crime and my charges. After looking over my file, he takes a deep breath and says, "These charges don't fit the crime. You're lucky that they didn't get you for all the charges that they put on you."

He sounds a little disappointed that they didn't.

Then he reads my charges out loud: "Attempted drug sale, and bribe receiving." And there's more. Then he says, "Well, I have some good news and some bad news. The good news is that since this is your first offense you qualify for a number of early-release programs, and the bad news is that I can't tell you which one of them they're going to send you to." I'm puzzled, so I ask, "Why is that? The judge gave me the Shock Program." He tells me that he'll look into it, because the officials up in Albany that run the prisons ultimately decide when and where an inmate gets housed. They don't give me or him that information for safety reasons.

"Safety reasons?" I ask.

"Yeah, if you and your people know when and where you are going to be moved, you could plan an escape," he says.

Sounds like BS to me. "You do realize that you're talking to a CO?" He says, "Well, believe me or not, that's the way it is." And just like that, our meeting is over. No answers whatsoever. I go back to my cell frustrated. I should have known that because of my high-profile status, I would be rejected for these early-release programs due to "safety reasons." A few days go by and I'm getting to know how things work here upstate.

You only get visits once a week, and you only get to call your family once a week. A lot of inmates write letters. I'm getting to know a few of the youngsters who are housed here with me. Amazingly, they also hang out with Rick, although they know all about his charges. One of the youngsters is Chris and the other is Junie. Chris is nineteen years old and acting like he's having the time of his life here in jail. He's always scribbling on his notepad, and when I ask him what he's writing he tells me that he's writing raps for his album that he'll put out once his appeal goes through. Okay. I'm all for being positive.

After lunch we all talk on the jack to one another, since our cells are right across from each other. Talking on the jack is lying on the floor and talking to each other through the bottom of our cell doors, which are about half a foot off the ground. This way we can see each other's face clearly and our conversations are more personal.

Junie says, "No disrespect, but how does it feel to be on this side?"

I shrug and say, "It's crazy but I made my bed and so I have to lie in it."

He says, "True." At this time a female CO walks by our cells to do a count and Chris sings out, "I'm in love with a stripper / she can pop it she can lock it." Junie just looks in his direction like he's crazy, shakes his head, then looks at me and says, "I don't know how this fool does it."

I ask, "What?"

He says, "Remain cool like we are about to go for a walk in the park. I'm stressing about all my shit and this fool over here is singing." I ask why he's stressing and he says, "I'm finished. I got fifteen to life for a body and guess what?"

"What?"

"I didn't do it."

I just gave him a nonjudgmental look and he continues. "I ain't going to lie, I ride for my set, but this shit ain't panning out the way it's supposed to. I'm here for taking the heat for my set and these niggas are supposed to be taking care of me and doing shit for my daughter on the outside but they ain't. I been down only a year and after I got sentenced I ain't heard or seen nobody from my set."

I ask him, "If you didn't do it, then why are you here?"

He says, "I ain't no snitch. I could have walked and all of that, the DA was going to cut me a deal if I told him who really bodied that kid, but I ain't no snitch."

I ask, "Have you heard from your family?"

He says, "Only the ones that I ain't shit on when I was out. My momma writes every now and then and I don't really get any visits or packages."

I can see the pain in his face; then he looks away from me as if he's thinking about his situation.

Chris looks at him and says, "Suck it up, nigga. You knew what it was when you decided to ride. I am a soldier for me and my niggas and I'm going to rep my hood till my casket drop."

Junie looks in his direction again and says, "Man, I have a four-year-old daughter!"

Chris comes back and says, "And? You knew you had her when

you was outside rolling, so now what's the point in dwelling on it? Shit is done."

I look at Junie and can tell that he doesn't want to hear what Chris is saying even though it is the truth. Junie then lays into Chris. "Nigga, you sitting there like this is some kind of joyride. These fools out there living it up at mine and your expense. They ain't riding for us. They ain't doing what they said that they were going to do. Look at you; the only one I see coming up here on a visit for you is your stressed-out moms. Where is all them other niggas at? Where they at?" He pauses for a response. Then Chris asks him, "Yo, what's good with you? Why you breaking down like this?" Junie flings him a letter that he just received and Chris reads it then flings it back. Chris, referring to the letter, says, "That ain't about nothing. You knew that bitch was going to fuck as soon as you got locked up. That's a part of this jail shit. Some chicks just ain't built for it. My chick ain't fucking, she's sitting there waiting on Daddy."

Junie again responds, agitated, "Muthafucka, I don't care about the bitch. It's the fact that my homeys who are supposed to be friends, that I am riding for, are now fucking her. Where's the loyalty? When you're out there hustling and busting your gun doing all types of stupid shit for these niggas it's all good, but as soon as you get knocked three months later they forget about you like you never did shit for them."

Chris is now pissed. He says, "Man up and quit your bitching." Junie yells back, "Man up? Man up? I know you just didn't say that stupid shit to me. Yo dumb ass in here for the same reason I'm in here, for following some dumb muthafucka ordering you to commit crimes that they ain't going to take the heat for. I bet you was the dolja nigga, the stupid nigga that was carrying the guns and the drugs for niggas. You was the first one to pop when they gave the order, the first one to make a move, and then when the heat came down you're the one that's locked up in here just like me. You sitting here singing that I am in love with a stripper shit to the CO like you don't have a sentence of fifty to life sitting on your chest."

He stops and shakes his head. I give a look of shock at the numbers he just threw out there. Then he continues. "You're cheesing around here talking about being a rapper when you get out, thinking that appeal of yours will happen overnight. Those shits don't work like that and especially if your family doesn't have money like that. They take years."

He laughs at Chris, whose attitude has turned serious, then says, "If your appeal works it will still be about ten years for them to even reduce your charges because you're not getting off scot-free and if it doesn't work you're talking fifty years before you're eligible for parole."

He pauses and acts like he's counting on his fingers, then says, "Ya nineteen and by the time you get out, granted they let you get parole at your first board, you will be damn near seventy something. Tah, and you think that bitch of yours ain't fucking? Let me school you, El Stupido, when you're in jail and doing a lot of time, the best thing that you can hope for out of a woman is for her to have enough respect for you to lie to you. If you got a woman who is accepting your collect calls, bringing you packages, visiting and writing you and still telling you that she loves you even though she's out there getting her rocks off, then you have a good woman. What woman in her right mind is going to wait fifty years? Shit, they ain't waiting fifty minutes. As soon as that hammer drops so do those panties."

He chuckles, because earlier Chris was getting at him, but he knows he has now successfully fucked up Chris's whole day. After that we continued to lie there on the floor in our cells, thinking about what happens next.

CHAPTER 55

TONNIE

The weekend arrives and I'm called for a visit. I'm escorted throughout the jail by two COs everywhere I go. I arrive at the visitors' floor looking for either my mother or my sister. Instead, I see a good friend of mine, Tonnie, sitting at a table with a pile of White Castle hamburgers in front of her. I'm happy and sad at the same time. Happy to see her, but sad she sees me like this. We hug and she smiles. I can sense an I-can't-believe-you're-in-prison vibe coming from her. I jump right in and explain to her why I did what I did. As I'm talking I'm also thinking that I will have this same conversation with others who care for me and expected more of me. Tonnie was beautiful, smart, and the type of woman who held her own. None of the big booty freaks that I rocked with came to see me. They didn't do the jail thing. Tonnie was different. She was a true friend. Though I didn't want anybody to come see me, I am glad she made the trip.

I am quiet at times while we are chatting. I find myself reflecting on how I was living as a CO and how blinded I became. Tonnie was a good woman and I never treated her properly because I was always chasing less deserving women. Her visit is humbling because I know she is here because she genuinely loves and cares for me, and that people come to visit an inmate because they want to. I know I can't just say to her, "Hey, I didn't want you when I was the high-and-mighty CO but now that I've ruined my life and lost everything let's be together." That would sound real stupid. But she tells me that she will stand by me as a friend for now and that we will see how everything works out. Before my visit is over, she says that she believes that I can overcome this and still make it when I get out. Hearing her say that to me gives me more inspiration to do whatever I need to do to get out of here. When she gets up to leave we hug and she feels so good that I don't want to let her go. But I have to. I realize the only bad thing about getting visits is when it is time for the visitor to leave. Tonnie's visit leaves me in good spirits. She is in my corner, and for the first time I think about how I need to do right by her when I get out.

The escort officer comes and picks me up and we begin to walk back to my housing area. He orders me to stop at the beginning of a long corridor. He radios ahead to another officer at the other end that I am coming. From the radio I hear the officer say, "Send him." Then the officer tells me to go. The officer stays behind as I begin to walk toward the other end. I'm high off my visit and I'm paying no attention to the other inmate that's walking toward me from the other end of the corridor. I can't take my mind off the smell of perfume on my hand. I'm halfway down the corridor when, *Wham!*

I'm hit on the side of my forehead. I stumble against the wall and quickly try to regain my bearings. I come out of my daze in time to see No-Joke, the inmate that Flocko cut for me. He has a scar on his face. He's squatting down with his hands in the back of his pants, and shits out a banger, which is a sharp object like an icepick. He lunges at me, but I catch his wrist. He's a little taller than me but luckily for me I outweigh him. As I continue to hold his arm, I hit him in the face a few times. We fall on the floor and begin to roll around. He's hell-bent on trying to wiggle his arm free so he can cut me. Now I hear footsteps of the officers coming down the corridor. I'm still wrestling with him, holding his arm tight, when he says, "You thought I wasn't going to remember your ass." The officers arrive and see that I have his wrist and that he has the weapon in a tight grip. They grab the banger from him and wrestle us apart. We are handcuffed and ordered to face the wall on our knees and not move. I'm breathing hard. All I keep thinking is that this muthafucka just tried to kill me! Officers order me to take off my shirt and part of my greens so they can see if I have been poked. They don't find anything, so they escort me to the clinic anyway because the hole could be real small and I could be bleeding internally and no one would know it.

While I'm in the clinic I keep replaying No-Joke saying that he remembered me. Protective custody don't mean shit if people really want to get to you. I'm deep in thought when a sergeant walks in and asks me if I'm okay. I tell him I'm fine.

"Listen," he says, "I am not going to write you up for fighting because of who you used to be but I need you to let this go." I look at him confused, because I know that this guy came at me and that they recovered the weapon from his hand, so why would I be in trouble? He says, "I know you know that Officer Stanton dropped the ball and that you were not supposed to be in that corridor by yourself. He was supposed to walk you all the way back to your area—the lazy fuck." I nod in acknowledgment but really I didn't know. He says, "So, we got a deal? I don't write you up and ruin what chances you may have at early release and you keep quiet about this."

I agree because I feel that I don't really have a choice. I don't want anything interfering with my going home early. The sergeant tells me that they will take care of No-Joke because they don't tolerate slashings and stabbings up here.

After I'm treated, I'm properly escorted to my area. When I get inside my cell I just sit up on the edge of my bed, with my hands clasped in front of my face, thinking about this whole jail situation. I'm thinking about this fool No-Joke who had the balls to attack me right there out in the open. Did he want to kill me that bad that he didn't care where we were or who was around? I come to the conclusion that this is going to happen everywhere I go, because I can't even begin to count the number of inmates that I put hands on for the sake of the job or for the sake of hustling. All the shit that I did can come back to me while I'm incarcerated. And what about my mother, my kids, my family, and now possibly Tonnie? I know I have to get through this. It's nobody's fault that I'm here but mine. I made my bed and now I have to lie in it. So I do just that. I lie down and go to sleep.

A few weeks later . . .

I'm told to pack up. I'm on the move again and I haven't received a word from my counselor. I have no idea where I'm going. Is it the Shock Program? Or maybe it's a minimum-security camp farther upstate. They have me in a cell in the intake area waiting to be transported. Across from me in another cell I see Chris. He's there with a bunch of other inmates eating off trays of food. Chris is not eating, though. He just has his food on his lap, staring out into space, looking dazed. I call out to him. He turns and looks at me. I ask him how his appeal is coming along. He doesn't say a word, just shakes his head. He has a look on his face that I've seen many times before. Reality has set in. He's never going home.

CHAPTER 56

ONEIDA

"Johnson, Peterson, Jones." A CO calls out inmates who will be getting off at this particular jail. The bus pulls off and we're on the road again.

I've been riding on the prison bus for a few hours, still with no clue as to where I'm going. Finally I hear my name called. I get up and shuffle my feet to the front of the bus. At this stop, I'm the only one getting off. I'm escorted into a van. Then it pulls off.

As we near the destination I survey the surroundings. It looks like a large college campus, a lot of grass and a lot of buildings and gates. We pull up to a building that looks real old but clean. The grass has been cut and the hedges trimmed. There's a porch in front where two COs are standing. I'm taken out of the van and made to stand in front of the two officers so they can inspect me as they go over my paperwork. One of them looks at me, leans his head to the side, and spits. Some of it hits the ground but some is still hanging off his lip. He says to me, "You're a big boy. Welcome to Oneida. Am I going to have any trouble out of you?" I say, "No." He then says, "You heard of Rick Jacobs, the guy that is in the papers for a hate crime against blacks?" I say, "Yes, I was just with him downstate." Then he asks, "Did you have a problem with him?" I answer, "No." He continues,

"Good, because his codefendant is here and we don't want any problems."

They escort me up some steps and into a cell. When they ask me if I have any questions for them I ask about when I can see a counselor. One of them answers, "He will be here first thing in the morning."

They allow me a phone call so that I can tell my family where I am. I call Moms and she has a million questions for me. "Are you at Shock? Are they sending you to Work Release?" She's just as excited as I am. I tell her I've just arrived here and that I won't find out anything until tomorrow. She keeps talking and asking questions but I tell her that I have to go. That night back in my cell I can't sleep. I'm anxious and I can't stop thinking that I've finally arrived at a place where I can get some answers.

Early the next day, my cell opens and I'm called out to see the counselor. I walk into a room with a white gentleman sitting on one side of a table with a folder in one hand and a cup of coffee in the other. He motions for me to sit down. He says, "I'm going to talk and tell you everything you need to know. Please don't interrupt me. This won't take but a second." I nod. He then says, "You have been sentenced to two years and have been sent here to Oneida Correctional Facility's Protective Custody Unit due to your high-profile case and the position of corrections officer that you held."

Then he drops the bomb. "Although this is your first offense and you qualify for many early-release programs, you will not be afforded any of them here because they require you to have a certain number of points. In order to get the points you have to be programming here first and we don't have any programs for you to take in the Protective Custody Unit." He then grabs my folder, gets up, and leaves.

"Wait a minute. I have some questions."

He turns and looks at me. "I just told you everything that you need to know." I'm panicked, because it was like he wasn't going to answer any of my questions. I ask him, "What about the Shock Program or the Work Release Program?" He looks at me like I am stupid and says, "Did you not just hear what I said? You're not getting any of them. You're going to do the rest of your time right here in PC."

"But the judge said that I could get Shock if it's available for me."

He looks puzzled, then turns to walk out of the room. He yells back at me, "I didn't see that in your folder. I have to look into it." And like that he was gone.

"Uh-oh, here comes trouble." I haven't done anything but the CO feels the need to say something when I return to my cell because he can tell that I'm angry. For the first time since I've been in jail, I want to be locked in. I want to be isolated. All I can feel is pain and rage. I have enough points to get Work Release and the judge recommended the Shock Program for me, but somehow, some way, I have to do the full two years.

I'm sitting on the edge of my bed and my eyes begin to swell up. I vow that I am not going to cry. I'm not going to crumble again. I take a deep breath and lie down thinking about my family, about how my mother is going to feel this. I have to convince her that I'll be alright and that everything is still okay. I decide I won't tell her right away, that we're still trying to figure out the whole thing. Technically, the counselor did say that he would check on the Shock Program.

A few days pass and I slowly begin to open up and talk to a few inmates. I know all about protective custody and the type of inmate that gets placed in it. I know that you have your rapists, your pedophiles, and ex–gang members that have dropped their flags. I make it my business to try not to find out anybody's charges, but in this place everybody talks. Many of them were COs like me, some state, some federal; some raped little girls, some raped little boys. I have to be mentally strong if I have to sit down and eat at the same table with some of these dudes. In the past, when I was a CO and I found out why they were here, I would've been judge, jury, and executioner. But now we're all incarcerated together.

I meet an older Muslim inmate named Paul who tells me about the procedures in the jail. He explains to me that they say that no one can sign out of Oneida's Protective Custody Unit once they're here, but he's seen different. He tells me that I'm not the right color. Paul is here for murder. He tried to rob somebody and when he showed his weapon, the victim fainted, hit his head on the curb, and died. Jason, Rick's hate crime codefendant, disagrees with Paul. He says he's seen several inmates get programming and go home. I just sit there absorbing everything that's being said.

The next day I ask to speak to the counselor, and when he comes I question him about finding the Shock Program. His response is "By the time you get the paperwork from the judge proving that he gave you the Shock Program, your two years will be up and you'll be home." He continues, "You have a Work Release board coming up. Maybe they will send you there."

There was still a glimmer of hope. Maybe I can still get out of here early.

More days pass and I finally receive notification that I'm to go before a board to determine whether I will be allowed to go to Work Release. I did my research and I know that I have more than enough points to go to this program.

On the morning of my board, I shave my head and I put on my cleanest green uniform. I psych myself up, thinking that if I look well kempt, they will see that I'm fit for the Work Release Program.

I get escorted to an office building. I'm told to go in and sit outside an office in the hallway until they call for me. I say the Lord's Prayer as I wait.

"We're ready for you now."

Inside the office I'm instructed to sit in a chair facing three people, two white ladies and one white gentleman. One of the ladies reads my charges out loud and then they start asking me a series of questions like "Why did you do it? Do you have any regrets or remorse for doing it? If you had the chance, what would you do differently?"

I answer them as professionally and as humbly as I can. The two ladies tell me that I'm a prime candidate for Work Release and that they will recommend me to the superintendent. I'm feeling good. I have a Kool-Aid smile on my face and everything. Finally, someone will have some sympathy for me and see that I really just made a mistake. Then one of the ladies asks the man who had been sitting there quietly throughout the whole interview does he have any questions for me. He says, "Yes, just one. How long were you doing it before you got caught?"

CHAPTER 57

LESSON LEARNED

I was told that the board normally takes two or three days before they make a decision. When I got back to my cell after the hearing a letter was waiting for me. My decision had already been made. It was as if the board already knew they weren't going to give me Work Release before they decided to question me. And still no answers from the counselor about the Shock Program. I'm frustrated. I dig deep and convince myself that this is just how things work when you've lost your rights. And I know that I'm expected to handle it the right way because I'm a former law enforcement officer. No matter who you are, when you break the law you're treated the same as everybody else. This is showing me that if you break the law as a law enforcer they're going to make sure you serve all the time that you were given. I know that the sergeant from the parole board probably felt that I should have gotten more time for this crime, so he was not going to let me just slide out of prison that easily.

I went before several boards over the next couple of months, each for a different early-release program. The reason for denial was always the same: "The seriousness and the nature of my crime." I realized that the judge can recommend anything but it's up to the people in Albany to decide what's going to happen to you if you're

265

incarcerated in New York City. I began to see some white inmates who were former corrections officers get the sex offender program, which would send them home early. This made me upset. I tried to sign out and take the risk of being housed in general population. In general population I could get some type of programming that would qualify me for Work Release. But I was always denied, with the excuse that no one can sign out of Oneida's Protective Custody Unit. I fought back by writing the superintendent of the jail, and Albany, questioning why the white ex-CO sex offenders get to sign out and receive programming, but the black ex-CO drug dealer has to stay and do all his time when he qualifies for every early-release program that's available.

I started documenting everything that was happening, from my denials to the names and numbers of the protective custody inmates who got to sign out. If I was ever asked to back up my claim of discrimination I wanted to have some credible information.

There was one situation when an inmate in protective custody was granted permission for Work Release. He was a relative of one of the people who decide who could or could not stay in protective custody. The inmate was white, and he was an ex–corrections officer. Now I was sure that Albany discriminates. I couldn't see it any other way. I was a CO. He was a CO. I was a safety risk for the facility. He was a safety risk for the facility. The only difference between the two of us was that he was white. I wrote his name and numbers down so that I could have that as an example for the lawsuit that I was about to file. I chuckled to myself, because when I was a CO I remember hearing inmates threaten to sue the department over their rights being violated or abused and now here I am trying to do the same thing. I never cared if they threatened to sue because I knew how difficult it was and most of the time the inmate, who made only seventeen cents a day, was too broke to pay for processing.

Some time has passed and my days are becoming routine. I begin to lift weights but I'm really not into it. I could care less about coming home all muscled up.

Occasionally I'll sit and talk with a few inmates. One day I'm talking to Paul and he begins to tell me about his wife, who he met on the visitors' floor. He tells me that he was on a visit with a family member and she was up there seeing someone with a girlfriend of hers. He says that they stared at each other the whole visit and that when the guy that her friend was visiting went to the bathroom, he went to the bathroom also and gave him his address to give to her. They've been together ever since. He says that they have two babies and that in the other jail he was in he managed to get her pregnant twice while having sex on the visitors' floor. Then he says something that throws me for a loop. He tells me that last year they took a vacation together, that they went to Hawaii and had a good time. I raise my eyebrows in disbelief, because he's here on a sixteen-to-life bid and has already served twenty-eight years.

He has me wait right where I am while he goes to the pictures to prove it. When he returns he opens up a scrapbook and shows me the pictures. He starts to narrate what happened on the trip, where they slept and all that. I take my eyes off the photos and look at him to see if he's serious. He is. While he is talking, Jason, the hate crime codefendant, who's sitting behind him, looks at me and waves his hand under his chin indicating I shouldn't say anything. Jason mouths to me that if I do Paul will want to fight. I look at the photos one more time to make sure that what I am seeing is the real thing. All the while Paul is talking nonstop about the trip. Then Paul gets up and says, "I'm going to show you the year before when we went to California." Then he gets up and leaves. At this point I know Paul has some serious mental issues. He is believable, but when you look at the scrapbook all you see are pictures of him and his wife cut out and pasted on a photo of Hawaii. Before Paul comes back Jason whispers to me that Paul lives and breathes for these pictures, so please don't get him started by telling him that he didn't go to these places. I laugh and get up to go to the bathroom. I look back at Jason and say, "Yeah, okay."

Then all of a sudden someone from behind me has put me in a choke hold. I struggle with my attacker and try to loosen his hold around my neck. We both fall to the ground and I manage to get loose. I stand up and see that it's a new inmate who has been here only a couple of days. We are both breathing hard and he's now blocking the doorway. Then he goes into his pocket and pulls out a shank. I can see in his eyes that he is high. He keeps mumbling to himself, repeatedly saying that he has to do this. I have no defense for the knife, so I take a stance and prepare myself to try and grab the knife before he can cut me. Before he's able to attack, COs bust through the door and grab him. They're trying their best to wrestle the knife out of his hand, but it seems like this inmate is a little too strong for them. Finally they manage to pry it loose and handcuff this crazy muthafucka.

By this time I know the routine. I'm already lying on the floor with my hands behind my head. They cuff me and take me back to my cell and lock me in. I sit there thinking about this second attempt on my life. At the same time I hear officers outside in the corridor talking about how high that inmate was. I start to remember how many times I'd gotten inmates high just like that while I worked the seven-to-three tour. I'd go home after my shift and the incoming officer had to deal with a high and crazed inmate. Little did they know, the inmate was high from drugs I supplied. For the very first time my actions then were staring me right in my face. A lot of people—inmates, officers—could've gotten hurt because of what I did for several years.

As I'm reflecting on everything I come to one conclusion. God is punishing me for my actions, not only for selling the drugs but for everything. For the way that I was living, period. For the way that I treated my mother, my kids, and the people who were around me. For the way I sexed some of my fellow officers' wives behind their backs. Everything. It just seems like I'm now paying for all the wrong I'd done. After a while I go to use the bathroom. I have no tissue, so I go to the window of my cell to get the attention of the officer on duty. I call out to him and ask if I can have some tissue. He waves me off and keeps walking, then yells back, "Wipe your ass with your hand!"

CHAPTER 58

NEVER AGAIN

"Oh, baby, don't stop, don't stop!"

I'm in the parking lot of Rikers Island and I have a female CO riding me in the back of my van. I'm grinding myself deep inside her when her cell phone rings. She reaches for it to see who it is. She says to me, "It's him. I have to answer." She doesn't dismount. I wait until she starts talking to her husband, then I start to grind inside her some more. She hits me on my chest for me to stop. I don't and it starts feeling good to her. Her eyes roll back in her head and she drops the phone and begins to say my name over and over again. "Oh, Heyward. Oh, Heyward!" Then it becomes just "Heyward! Heyward!"

I open my eyes and realize that I was dreaming. I was still a CO in the dream. I have a grip on myself that would make a boa constrictor proud. Even more embarrassing is that a CO is standing in the window of my cell shining a light on me. He's laughing and waving his hand back and forth. He tells me to get dressed and informs me that I'm needed to move some property. I get up, wash my hands, and throw on my greens. It's the middle of the night and I'm wondering what inmate property has to be moved right now. The officer tells me to follow him. We walk over to the next floor, to the unit above mine. He orders me to bag up all the inmate's property that's in cell 3. All this seems kind of strange, so I ask him, "Why am I doing this now in the middle of the night?" The CO says, "The inmate just hung himself and we need his stuff packed and inventoried." I stand there for a minute in the doorway of this tomb looking around and taking in the view. I begin to pack the inmate's stuff. I overhear the COs in the corridor talking about the inmate just being some young punk who couldn't do his time and took the easy way out. Then one says to the other, "Hey, look at it this way, he beat those charges."

That comment made me furious. Inmate or not, this person was a human being and even if he was to live the rest of his life in prison he still deserved a little empathy. I continue to clean and pack his cell. I start to reflect on all the inmates who I came into contact with when I was a CO. We made decisions that landed us in a system that controls us. That's the main ingredient of jail: control. Naturally, when we become adults we own our actions. We decide whether we're going to make a right turn or a wrong turn. If our actions go against the laws put before us then it is determined we must be controlled. That's where jail comes in. It not only confines you physically, but it confines your choices. No longer can you eat, sleep, and drink when you want. No longer are you a free citizen.

Some feel that jail is modern-day slavery because of the way inmates are treated. I beg to differ, because even though inmates get beaten unjustly sometimes and they are forced to do things against their will, those inmates, before getting locked up, decided to do wrong. Slaves did not have such an option. When you break the law and get caught, you put yourself at the mercy of an unfair court system and corrections officers who, at times, have the power to be judge, jury, and executioner. And the legal system puts considerably more effort into governing inmates than it puts into governing the behavior of corrections officers. This creates an atmosphere where the few rights an inmate has often get violated but there is little justice for them.

As I finish packing the deceased inmate's belongings, I also think about other inmates who may feel like taking their life is the only way out. Jail can do that to you.

Prison should be feared at all times. As corny as it may sound, prison should be thought about every time a person thinks about doing something wrong. Now I know incidents happen that sometimes unjustly land someone in prison. Things like wrong-place-wrong-time can't always be avoided. But at all costs, jail should be avoided. Jail is not a badge of honor. There is nothing glorious about being controlled. No one is invincible inside these walls. I've witnessed even the toughest person get backed down and beat. For every person out there that thinks he's tough there are, at minimum, thousands of inmates that will prove to him otherwise.

I drag his belongings out of the cell and I vow to myself that once I get released I'm never coming back here again.

Months pass and it's time for me to be released. I'm thankful that I had only a twenty-month sentence. I know it could've been much worse. The day before my release a CO hands me a letter from Albany, and when I open it, I read that they are now granting me Work Release. I shake my head. All along I could've gone to Work Release and all the talk about my being in protective custody and the serious nature of my crime was just crap. Albany just didn't want me to get out early. I guess now they can officially say that they gave me Work Release so it will appear that they don't discriminate. At this point I'm over it anyway. I fold the paper up and put it away so that when I look at it again it'll remind me that never again will I come back to this place.

EPILOGUE

When I get home, I'm greeted by my son, who has now outgrown me. His cell phone rings and it's my mother checking to see if he has seen me yet, because everyone is awaiting my arrival.

I enter the apartment and I'm greeted by my mother, who holds me tight for a very long time, and the tears just start rolling down her face and mine. All I feel is the unconditional love that she has for me. I can also feel the pain that I've caused her. I know that as usual I owe her a debt that I can never repay.

The next day I report to my parole officer. He gives it to me straight, letting me know that I have an uphill battle ahead of me. He tells me that jobs are tight, that we're in a recession, and that I have a felony conviction as an ex–law enforcement person and that I lost a city job. He tells me that as a part of my parole conditions, it's mandatory to get employment, and if I fail to do so I can be sent back to prison. I take in everything he's saying. I'm positive, because I know that I will do whatever it takes to make things right again. If I have to work two fast-food jobs, I will. It don't matter. All that matters right now is that I'm home and here is my second chance.

While I was in prison, I had my mom apply for a job on my behalf. They sent her a letter back stating that I qualified and when the hiring process would start. When my parole officer sees the letter he tells me that he might have to stop me because the job was a good one, which means that I could get back on my feet sooner rather than later, and thus start selling drugs again. *Isn't a parole officer supposed to encourage you to get a job and get back on your feet as soon as possible? Besides, I don't need a good-paying job to sell drugs again.* Nevertheless, he lets me go to the orientation and that's when I find out just how the prosecuting DA did me dirty.

My charges were attempted drug sale in the third degree and bribery receiving in the third degree. When an employer looks at my application, he will see the more serious charge first, the drug sale charge. In this day and age, with that charge, an employer may be willing to take a chance and give me a job. However, once he sees the bribery charge, the employer may scratch his head and figure that the normal Joe Blow standing-on-the-corner hustler is not going to get that type of charge. So the employer is now prompted to ask me what kind of position I held that would put me in a position to be bribed. Once I tell him my story, trying to be truthful and not lie, my interview is over. So that was the last dagger that the system gave me: Let's make it hard for him to get employed again and maybe he will slip up again and land back in prison.

Long story short, that didn't happen. In fact, to show how good God is, upon completing my parole obligation, not only did I land a job, I landed another city job with a pension and benefits. Today I walk around as an example to let people know that you can bounce back from anything, and just because you went to jail, it's not the end of the world.

HOW TO PREVENT A CORRUPT CORRECTIONS OFFICER

1. Perform random strip searches on officers as they enter the facility, or at least randomly pat them down. An officer will think twice about bringing in contraband if the threat of a random search looms.

2. Perform random locker searches and make sure they're on the same day as the strip search. Once again, you want officers thrown off guard and unable to predict when a search will take place.

3. Make it mandatory that officers who man the front gate post are from another jail. Also, use a supervisor from another jail to oversee what happens at the front gate. This helps eliminate camaraderie and favoritism among officers as they enter.

4. When an inmate housing area is being searched by a drug dog, make sure the dog also sniffs out the officers' station. This will prevent an officer from hiding contraband inside the officers' station if an officer knows a search is coming for his or her housing area.

5. Randomly send officers down to the inspector general's office for questioning even if the officers are not accused of anything. Have the inspector general ask them about the jail. Notify officers at roll call so that they know that they will be questioned. Officers will say anything in a confidential setting with pressure coming from the inspector general. Officers will be cautious about doing anything illegal if they know that there is a chance another officer will give them up.